HUDDERSFIELD
the trolleybus years

BY STEPHEN LOCKWOOD

Contributions by David Beach and Philip Jenkinson

Maps by Roger Smith

Published by Adam Gordon

COVER PHOTOGRAPHS

FRONT COVER

Trolleys in John William Street, 1965. (Fred Ivey)

REAR COVER

Upper: A scene at Ainley Top in 1939. The vehicle is in the original trolleybus livery of two shades of red. (From an original painting by Robert Nixon in the author's collection)

Lower: This atmospheric night-time shot at a wintry Fixby terminus shows no. 589 awaiting departure time on a through journey to Almondbury. This was the inaugural date of route 34. 31 January 1963. (Alan Dixon/Paul Watson)

TITLE PAGE

Trolley no. 578 is seen leaving Elland town centre in 1958. (Peter Mitchell)

A busy scene at Westgate in 1959 showing trolley no. 476, which by this time was one of only two entirely pre-war vehicles still in operation. (Vic Nutton, colour added by Malcolm Fraser)

ISBN 978-1-910654-00-2

Publication no. 104

Published in 2015 by Adam Gordon, Kintradwell Farmhouse, Brora, Sutherland KW9 6LU

Tel: 01408 622660

E-mail: adam@ahg-books.com

Printed by: Henry Ling Ltd (The Dorset Press, Dorchester DT1 1HD)

Production by: Trevor Preece, 2 Sella Bank, The Banks, Seascale, Cumbria CA20 1QU

E-mail: trevor@trpub.net

CONTENTS

Taking the trolley into town. Trolley no. 542, coming up Newsome Road from the terminus, approaches the stop at Castle Avenue. (Vic Nutton, colour added by Malcolm Fraser)

AUTHOR'S NOTE

This book, describing one of the most loved trolleybus systems in Britain, was originally intended to be an album of photographs, mainly in colour, describing all the routes in turn. However the publisher felt that the subject deserved a broader treatment, and accordingly a substantial historical based section has been added. This is an illustrated historical review using black and white images, which is followed by the all-colour route-by-route photographic survey.

Huddersfield's trolleybus history has been fully recorded in the past by the town's foremost public transport expert, the late Roy Brook in his definitive 1976 work *The Trolleybuses of Huddersfield*. It is not my intention to emulate or replace this (and indeed I have consulted his book during the compilation of the historical review), but to complement it by showing what Huddersfield and its environs were like when the trolleys ran throughout the area. I have tried to use illustrations that have not been previously published, and indeed, apart from a very small number that have appeared in trolleybus enthusiast magazines, all the colour views are shown here for the first time.

One of the many delightful aspects of compiling this work has been the enthusiastic co-operation shown by the many contributors, all of whom have gone out of their way to accommodate me. The photographers are credited individually in each caption, but I wish to mention individuals whose help has been invaluable. Firstly, I need to thank Tony Belton who asked me to privately caption his Huddersfield trolleybus photographs, and it was this exercise that was the genesis of this album. My good friend Paul Watson not only provided black and white views from the Roy Brook and Jim Copland collections, but also made available a cache of colour slides originally taken by the late Alan Dixon. Paul arranged for these slides to be skilfully enhanced by Tony Harman of Maple Leaf Images, Newmarket Street, Skipton BD23 2JB. Martin Jenkins and Peter Waller of the Online Transport Archive provided many images from that collection, including some very rare early 1950s colour views. Mike Russell sent me vast numbers of views taken between 1965 and 1968 and David Clarke allowed me the use of his interesting selection of slides which covers the closing years of the system. Others who supplied Huddersfield views to select from are Don Akrigg, Roland Box, Carl Isgar, Fred Ivey, Malcolm King, Bruce Lake, John Laker, the late Stan Ledgard, Alan Murray-Rust, David Pearson, Geoff Smith and Tony Wilson of Travel Lens Photographic (Vic Nutton photographs). Transport artist Robert Nixon has kindly allowed me to reproduce his painting of a trolleybus at Ainley Top on the rear cover.

The maps have been drawn by Roger Smith in his usual thorough style, and these include some chronology maps as well as the wiring plans.

Other important contributors are David Beach and Phillip Jenkinson, both Huddersfield born, who have contributed items of text on conducting experiences and the Introduction respectively. Philip, together with another native of the town, Peter Cardno, has read through the text and captions. Malcolm Fraser has coloured some of the black and white images. David Hall and Hugh Taylor have also provided valuable assistance.

Sincere thanks go to all the above. Finally I need to thank my wife Eileen for checking the text with a 'non-enthusiast' eye, and for her patience when I frequently disappeared for an hour or so to put this work together.

Stephen Lockwood
Darlington
November 2014

BIBLIOGRAPHY

These works have been consulted during the compilation of this book:
The Trolleybuses of Huddersfield, Roy Brook, 1976
Huddersfield Corporation Tramways, Roy Brook 1983
Reading Trolleybuses, D.A. Hall, Trolleybooks, 1991
Huddersfield – a most handsome town, E.A.H. Haigh (ed), Kirklees Cultural Services, 1992
Sunbeams and Showers, Philip Jenkinson, (unpublished), 2001
Huddersfield Trolleybuses, Stephen Lockwood, Middleton Press, 2002
Huddersfield – the Corporation Motorbus Story, Cardno and Harling, Robin Hood Publishing, 2003
Huddersfield Tramways – The original Municipal System, Stephen Lockwood, Middleton Press 2007
The Trolleybus Museum at Sandtoft – Museum Guide and Handbook, Venture Publications, 2010

In Town and Beyond

The railway station, in the background of this view, was typical of the soot-stained buildings of the town centre during the trolleybus era. Fortunately it was cleaned as part of the Borough Centenary celebrations in 1968. The trolleybus, no. 545, received new East Lancashire bodywork in 1961, but did not last long in this state – it was withdrawn from service in October 1964 as a result of severe accident damage in Longroyd Bridge Depot. (Robert Mack)

Far from the urban bustle, the first post-war trolleybus, no. 541, is seen climbing The Ainleys on its way from Elland into town in the early 1960s. (Peter Mitchell)

FOREWORD

'On 13 July 1968, the public of Huddersfield gathered in their hundreds to witness the end of an era, and for many a lifetime's association with the trolleybus. In their heyday, the trolleybuses were synonymous with frequent services, safe and silent travel, fume free speedy journeys (especially uphill), and above all low fares. Their hill-climbing abilities made them the ideal vehicle for Huddersfield's steep gradients.'

These words, penned by Roy Brook in an article on Huddersfield's public transport which appeared in the book *Huddersfield – a most handsome town*, form a most appropriate appraisal of the subject.

The trolleys, as folk commonly referred to them (sometimes 'trolleybus' but never 'bus'), were part of the life in the town for 34 years. They were stately vehicles having double wheels at the rear, sporting a bright livery of red with cream, almost yellow, bands. The lowest of these swooped down at the front so that the panel under the windscreens was all cream, the town crest and the black fleet number being prominent here. No external advertising was allowed, so the trolleys were never plastered with banners about football pools or Hammonds Ales (the local brew).

The vehicles, and the overhead wiring which defined their operation, were very well maintained and the service was much loved by residents and trolleybus fans alike. The trolleys had their idiosyncrasies, such as the trolley poles occasionally leaving contact with the overhead wires, the conductor having to jump off to pull a handle (called the 'trigger') to allow the trolley poles to take the correct path at junctions and the interior lights winking off and on at night whenever the poles passed over a dead section. The affection for these vehicles is shown today by the frequent nostalgic photo features published in the Huddersfield daily newspaper *'The Examiner'*.

Much of the interest was the nature of the routes they travelled. To Marsden they ran along the Colne Valley with panoramic vistas across to the Pennine hills and moorland. From West Vale, there was the view over the Calder Valley at Hullen Edge, and the steep climb of The Ainleys where the trolleys romped up with ease. On the Outlane route they climbed to the highest trolleybus terminus in Britain, right on the edge of the Pennine moors. Even the shorter routes

within the town environment were impressive: at Longwood the trolleys traversed a hairpin bend, ran through the narrow village street, then reversed onto a special platform built out from the road at the terminus. In Birkby there was the big dipper-like switchback at Birkby Hall Road, where the trolleys ran down the hill and immediately climbed again to the other side of the valley beside Norman Park.

The trolleybus system, such a distinctive feature in the town during those years, is a far cry from today's public transport, run by private companies with their corporate liveries – much the same as in any other town up and down the country.

Corporation Motorbus Services

From 1930, Huddersfield's municipal motorbus fleet was a joint operation with the London, Midland and Scottish Railway Company (later British Railways). Even numbered buses were Corporation-owned and odd ones railway-owned. Policy was set by the Joint Omnibus Committee (JOC) and the service was known as the 'Joint Omnibus Services'. Management and staff were common between the wholly Corporation-owned tram fleet (later trolleybus) and the motorbus fleet. From 1961, when the first major trolleybus abandonment occurred, the motorbuses replacing the trolleys were wholly owned by the Corporation and carried a pseudo trolleybus livery with a cream swoop over the driver's cab. In 1969 the two fleets were merged and the Corporation assumed total control of the combined undertaking. This continued until 1974 when the undertaking was merged with the municipal bus fleets of Bradford, Halifax and Leeds to form the West Yorkshire Passenger Transport Authority.

A scene on the Birkby switchback. No. 598 is seen climbing Birkby Hall Road. The opposing gradient alongside Norman Park is visible in the background. (Peter Mitchell)

INTRODUCTION

A personal introduction to Huddersfield's trolleys by Philip Jenkinson

Back in the early 1950s, the Jenkinson family would often indulge in 'trips off'. 'Trips off' meant long rides, often to nowhere in particular, in Uncle George's car. This was large (or so it always seemed; its largeness may be a product of my memory, or it may be a reality coloured by the smallness of many modern cars; certainly it shouldn't be inferred that Uncle George's car was in any way grandiose, for it was not). It was, not entirely oddly at that time, also black; and it was an Austin. Beyond that I can't say much about George's car, except that it was an event when the vehicle touched 40mph, which was at the turn of the 1950s a not inconsiderable speed. George worked for Grandad, and the car came in useful for their joinery business, no doubt; but at weekends George's car became the liberating medium which some people still believe the car to be. It was true in 1951 in a way it certainly is not sixty years later.

Nevertheless, liberated though we felt we were, you always came home. And there was never any doubt about the moment, you knew. It might be as you entered Marsden at the bottom of the long descent from Standedge on Manchester Road. It might be as you completed the little climb up from Elland Bridge to the Town Hall on the way back from Halifax. It might come as you climbed away from Cooper Bridge on the way in from Leeds. I think in our case it might most often of all have been the moment you came up out of the dip at Tandem, with the old County Motors depot up on the hill on your left, and halted at the junction of Wakefield Road with Penistone Road.

But at all those places, you were welcomed back to Huddersfield by those twin sets of parallel overhead wires, which would always slink in from one side or the other, almost unnoticed unless, like me, you were looking for them. Suddenly you were under the wires that declared Our Town to be Somewhere, as opposed to pathetic little wireless towns like Halifax, Wakefield and Barnsley, which were quite clearly Nowhere.

And sooner rather than later, after settling comfortably under those wires, there would come the Defining Moment of being Home. No doubt at least partly to humour me, but I like to think partly out of a similar feeling of returning to the comforts of home, everyone in the car was looking out, eager to be the first one to spot a double-decker with poles on the roof. For home meant trolleybuses; big, red trolleybuses. Nowhere else seemed to have anything quite the same. I was always so proud of them.

Now it is true that other towns could claim to be Somewhere, notably nearby Bradford, where the trolleywires sometimes seemed to go on forever, especially if, as was often the case on a trip to the Dales, we travelled along Manningham Lane. But Bradford's trolleys were nippy little beggars; not the majestic personalities we had in Huddersfield. Our trolleybuses had that indefinable extra; they had class. And, of course, they were Ours. The real reason you knew you were home was because the Huddersfield trolleybuses could never really escape Huddersfield. They might venture seven miles out of town to Marsden in the Colne Valley, or strike boldly into the neighbouring boroughs of Elland and Brighouse, but ultimately, like me, they all had to come back home. They inspired a pride and loyalty which motorbuses owned by massive national bus groups could never hope to inspire.

I was born in a trolleybus town. And although I shall die in it after living over twice as long in a Huddersfield without trolleybuses than one with them, I shall never feel it to be other than a trolleybus town.

The first glimpse of a Huddersfield trolleybus might be as you entered Marsden at the bottom of the long descent from Standedge on Manchester Road. The wires turn from Fall Lane into Manchester Road, which runs left to right in this view. In 1955, no. 583 has reversed using a temporary reverser erected whilst roadworks prevented use of a turning circle at the terminus. (Roy Brook/Paul Watson)

THE STORY OF HUDDERSFIELD TROLLEYBUSES

1 Origins

A steam tram and trailer in Railway Street on 15 April 1892, prior to working the first journey to Salendine Nook after the rails were extended there from the Lindley route at Marsh. (Author's collection)

Steam Trams

The form and scope of the trolleybus system was directly related to the steam tram network that developed in the late 19th century. It is well known that the town was the first municipality to be allowed to operate its own tram system, due to the inability of the Corporation to lease its tracks to a private operator as the law required at the time. The steep terrain of the town was no doubt a great factor in bringing about this unwillingness.

Municipal steam trams commenced running between Fartown Bar and Lockwood Bar on 11 January 1883, and by 1900 there were 27 steam engines and 25 passenger cars to run on the 23-mile network. The track gauge was 4ft 7¾in. to allow railway wagons to operate on the tracks (running on their flanges), although this never happened.

One innovation introduced by the steam trams was the carriage of post-boxes where the public could post letters, and this facility carried on into the trolleybus era, lapsing at the outbreak of the Second World War.

STEAM TRAMS – ROUTE NETWORK AS AT 1900
Almondbury
Berry Brow via Lockwood
Birkby
Bradley
Crosland Moor
Honley (an extension of the Berry Brow route used
    by steam trams for 15 days only in June 1902.)
Longwood (Quarmby Clough)
Lindley and Edgerton circular via Holly Bank Road
Newsome Road (Stile Common)
Outlane
Sheepridge
Slaithwaite
Waterloo

Electric Traction

The electrification of street tramways was rife across the country at this time, Huddersfield being no exception. The steam tram routes were converted in two stages, starting on 14 January 1901 with the Outlane, Lindley and Edgerton routes (the latter two being linked along Holly Bank Road). The second stage took place in 1902, and when the route to Bradley opened on 13 July conversion was complete.

The first electric trams were 25 Milnes built bogie cars built in 1900. One of these is seen at Fartown Bar in the early years of electric traction with The Royal Hotel on the corner of Fartown Green Road in the background. The bogies were not suitable for Huddersfield use, owing to difficulties in fitting track brakes, and these were replaced within a few years by a four-wheel truck. The word 'electric' in the fleet title on the rocker panel did not last long either, not least because subsequent trams were shorter in length and this form of title would not fit. (Author's collection)

The electric tram system prospered, and many extensions to the original routes were opened, as well as doubling of the tracks. One notable innovation was a service, inaugurated in 1904, of coal-carrying to three local mills on the Outlane route. This used two specially built coal trams shuttling from the railway coal depot, just off Bradford Road at Hillhouse. The last tramway extension was from Smithy (on the Sheepridge route) to Brighouse, this incorporating a ¾-mile stretch of reserved sleeper track through the woods from Netheroyd Hill to Fixby. By early 1933 the fleet stood at 140 cars running over 37 miles of route. This total included eight luxury domed roof cars built by English Electric in 1931/2 which were deemed some of the finest tramcars of their type in the country.

ELECTRIC TRAMS – ROUTE NETWORK AS AT
    JANUARY 1931
(showing through services, and route numbers
    introduced in 1918)
1   Waterloo to Lindley
2   Newsome (Church) to St George's Square
3   Waterloo to Outlane
4   Bradley to Marsden
6   Crosland Moor (Dryclough Road) to St George's
    Square
7   Almondbury to West Vale
8   Dod-Lea (Longwood) to Birkby
9   Brighouse to St George's Square
10 Sheepridge to Honley
Note: route no. 5 was never used, and the tracks
    connecting Lindley and Edgerton were disused
    after the latter route's extension to Birchencliffe
    in 1911, although they remained in place.

This is one of the pair of coal-carrying trams introduced in 1904 which delivered coal from the railway at Hillhouse to three mills on the Outlane route. Initially given the next fleet numbers in the passenger car series (71 and 72), they were re-numbered 1 and 2 respectively in 1909 in their own series. They worked until shortly before the Outlane route was converted to trolleybuses in 1934.

The heyday of the trams is represented here by this view of New Street in about 1930, looking south from the Kirkgate junction towards Chapel Hill. Nearest the camera is car 136, the last of ten fully-enclosed English Electric cars dating from 1924. It is working on route 4 to Bradley and is followed by an open balcony car on route 8 to Birkby. (Commercial postcard – Author's collection)

2 The First Trolleybus Route – Almondbury

Trolleybus Powers

Not all of the 'luxury tramcars' had even entered service when the Tramways Committee, considering the costs of relaying the tram track on the Almondbury route, saw an opportunity to experiment with trolleybuses, or 'trolley vehicles' as they were then known. By the early 1930s, these vehicles had proved themselves elsewhere in the country to be practical successors to replace trams. Bradford (only 10 miles away), and Wolverhampton had already built up sizeable trolleybus systems to replace their trams, and a network in south-west London had just been inaugurated. Parliamentary powers to operate trolleybuses to Almondbury were sought and obtained in 1932. In December of that year work started to reconstruct the roadway between the tram terminus and the Wakefield Road junction at Aspley. The tram route was gradually cut back as work progressed.

The New Route

The new trolleybus wiring was quite simple in nature, there being no short working turning points along the route, and the terminus at Almondbury, like the trams, was at the junction of Northgate and Wormald Street, where a triangular reverser was provided into the latter street. In the town centre a loop was provided, turning off Kirkgate via Byram Street, (where the terminal stop was situated), St Peter's Street and Northgate, rejoining the main route at Southgate, which was then a new road only just completed. This ran parallel to the southern part of Kirkgate, (now known as Oldgate), which the Waterloo trams continued to use. A connection was provided along Northgate via Ray Street to Great Northern Street depot, where the six trolleybuses bought for the route were housed. In total the trolleybus wiring was just under 2½ miles in length.

The Trolleybus Era Begins

An opening ceremony took place on the morning of 4 December 1933, when two trolleybuses, one of which was no. 2, carried a civic party over the new route. Public services commenced in the early afternoon, when the temporary motorbus service was withdrawn. The route was allocated no. 65.

Ransomes trolleybus no. 1 has just arrived in Northgate, Almondbury in this view taken just after the inauguration of the route. Note the conductor delivering a parcel, a common feature of public transport at this time. (A.J. Owen)

Bus Terminus, Northgate.

This commercial postcard depicts the original layout of the reversing triangle at Almondbury trolleybus terminus. Vehicles drove into Wormald Street then reversed out into Northgate. The layout was altered during World War II to allow vehicles to reverse into Wormald Street, and in 1951 the route was extended a few yards along Northgate to a purpose-built turning circle. Note the narrow spacing (18") of the overhead wires. (Author's collection)

The New Vehicles – Trolleybuses nos 1 to 6

The six new trolleybuses were of differing chassis, body and electrical equipment manufacture, in order to test which were most suitable for operation in the town. They were numbered 1 to 6 in a new trolleybus fleet sequence. All were 60-seat six-wheeled double-deckers, this configuration being necessary because the Corporation wished the new vehicles to be able to match the capacity of the trams they replaced. In brief, the vehicles were:

1 Ransomes D6 chassis with Brush body
2 Karrier E6 chassis with Park Royal body
3 Karrier E6 chassis with Park Royal body
4 Sunbeam MS2 chassis with Park Royal body
5 Karrier E6 chassis with English Electric body
6 AEC 663T chassis with English Electric body

(Nos. 5 and 6 displayed the prefix 'No.', and this became the standard on all pre-war vehicles)

At the town centre terminus of the route, Karrier no. 3 stands on the stone setts in Byram Street. (Travel Lens Photographic)

The rear profile of Karrier no. 2 before entry into service. (Roy Brook collection / Paul Watson)

Scammonden and Lowerhouses – Trolleybus proposals that never came to fruition

In 1913, Huddersfield Corporation obtained powers to operate a trolleybus service from the Outlane tram terminus westwards along New Hey Road to the Borough Boundary at Scammonden. The Great War frustrated any progress and the powers eventually lapsed. It is difficult to see how such a service along a moorland road could be remunerative, although it would have made the Outlane terminus a very interesting place, with tramcars and trolleybuses as well as the coal-carrying trams to Gosport Mill, just beyond the terminus. When the Tramways Committee decided to run trolleybuses to Almondbury, they also resolved to include a route branching off Somerset Road along Longley Road to the junction of Hall Cross Road at Lowerhouses. The terminus would have been at the Mason's Arms. Strong opposition to this proposal from the residents of Longley Road meant that it never happened (Parliamentary powers not being applied for). The residents of Lowerhouses were eventually served by a motorbus route running via Dog Kennel Bank.

Sunbeam trolleybus no. 4 is seen on test in Somerset Road before the commencement of services. Unlike the previous views, this photograph brings out the lighter red on the upper bodywork. (Author's collection)

AEC no. 6 had an English Electric body and was the only Huddersfield trolleybus to have a single step on to the platform. This is demonstrated in this view of a passenger boarding the vehicle in the newly opened Southgate. The Oxford Hotel is in the background. (Author's collection)

Looking from Westgate, this view shows trolleybuses in Kirkgate. The nearer one is at the original main Lindley/Outlane stop. This was moved to the west end of Westgate in 1947. This scene dates from 1939, when major road works were taking place in this area. (W.E. Turton/Kirklees Cultural Services)

Trolleybuses for Outlane, Lindley and Waterloo

In the Spring of 1933, months before the inauguration of the trolleybuses, a new General Manager took the reins of the Tramways Department. He was Harry Godsmark, who had already gained considerable experience of trolleybuses at Nottingham. One of his first acts was to recommend to his Committee that necessary expenditure on the tram tracks of the Lindley and Outlane routes was not justified, and that trolleybuses should be substituted. This was before any experience had been gained of these vehicles being operated in the town. The necessary Parliamentary powers were applied for, and these included the Waterloo route. This made sense because the Lindley and Outlane routes were linked operationally across the town to Waterloo, and the Almondbury trolleybus wiring would already be in place over its route as far as the Lyceum junction at Aspley. To operate these routes, 24 additional trolleybuses were ordered, these being of the Karrier type, locally built in St Thomas Road, near to the tram depot at Longroyd Bridge.

The New Routes

Commencing operation on Armistice Day, 11 November 1934, these cross-town routes ran from the moorland village of Outlane in the west through the town to Waterloo in the east, with a short branch off the former route to Lindley.

There were short workings at Salendine Nook (with a triangular reverser), Marsh (a 'round the houses' loop), and on the Waterloo section at Moldgreen (Grosvenor Road), where the triangular reverser proved unsatisfactory and was replaced in 1936 by a one-way clockwise loop around Broad Lane, Grand Cross Road and Grosvenor Road. In the town centre wires were erected in Kirkgate and Westgate, the former being used in both directions. On eastbound journeys the trams had turned right at the Market Place onto New Street, then left into King Street, which now lost its public transport provision. Route numbers were allocated thus:

71 Lindley to Waterloo
72 Marsh to Moldgreen
73 Outlane to Waterloo
74 Town Centre to Salendine Nook

It should perhaps be mentioned here that it was the Corporation Transport practice, from when route numbers were introduced in 1918 until the end of its existence in 1974, that a vehicle displayed the route number of the terminus which it was operating to, regardless of where it was starting its journey from. For example, a service terminating at Salendine Nook but starting at Waterloo, would show '74' throughout. This also applied on services that were not otherwise linked, and an example of this is shown in the photograph on page 146 (centre photo).

No. 8 was a 1934-built Brush-bodied Karrier, seen here at the bodybuilders works before delivery. Note the fleet number shown as No. 8, the 'radiator' outline on the front dash panel and the experimental trafficators which were unique to this vehicle. (Author's collection)

The Fleet Grows – Trolleybuses nos 7 to 30

Like three of the original fleet, the 24 new vehicles had Karrier E6 chassis. The body order was split equally between Brush (nos 7 to 18) and Park Royal (nos 19 to 30). Visually, the main difference between the two types was that the Brush body incorporated a dummy radiator outline below the driver's windscreens, whilst the Park Royal body had a plain panel, allowing the central cream band to extend around the front. All had seats for 64 passengers.

Outlane terminus

At over 900 feet above sea level this was Britain's highest trolleybus terminus. It was exceeded only by Halifax's early trackless terminus at Wainstalls which reached over 1,000 feet, but this was a short-lived operation of five years (1921 to 1926), and therefore did not exist when Outlane welcomed its first trolley.

The first of the 1934 Park Royal bodied vehicles, no. 19 is seen here before delivery to Huddersfield. There was no 'radiator' on this batch, enabling the cream stripe to continue around the front below the cab. (Author's collection)

4 Trolleybuses Triumphant 1936 to 1940

The Trams are Doomed

The decision was made to convert all the remaining tram routes to trolleybus operation in the Spring of 1935. This entailed the promotion of a Parliamentary Bill, which in July 1936 was passed as the *Huddersfield Corporation (Trolley Vehicles) Act 1936*. It gave the Corporation general powers to run trolleybuses on all the tram routes, as well as some planned extensions. Also included was a diversionary route for the Brighouse route to avoid the sleeper tramroad section, although trolley vehicles could run on this if a new road was built along its formation and opened for all traffic. Another minor, although

This is no. 31, the experimental Karrier vehicle with all-metal Weymann bodywork. It is being tilt-tested at London Transport's Chiswick works. Note the Karrier and Weymann badges on the front dash panels. (Roy Brook collection)

interesting provision, was that the Act stipulated that trolley vehicles were required to keep to the left of the road.

Newsome was the first tram route to be converted following the passing of the Act, and for this eight additional Karrier trolleybuses were ordered.

Two Experimental Trolleys, nos 31 and 32

In the midst of all the planning for the mass conversion of tram routes, two 'one-off' experimental vehicles were purchased, entering service in the winter of 1935-6. Both vehicles were exhibited at the Commercial Motor Show at London in November 1935.

No. 31 was a Karrier E6 with a Weymann metal-framed 64-seat body. The all-metal construction meant that traction lighting could not be used, and this was the only trolleybus in the fleet whose lighting was uninterrupted when it passed over an insulator in the overhead wiring. Its appearance was more modern than previous deliveries.

No. 32, another Karrier, had a Park Royal body of traditional composite (wood/metal) construction. However, it was probably more significant than no. 31 because it was of a streamlined style, and in a livery with a cream swoop filling the space underneath the cab windscreens. It also had a three-section destination indicator layout at the front. This vehicle was essentially the prototype for the large fleet of vehicles needed to replace the trams.

Another interesting point about both these vehicles was that they were the first in the fleet to have coasting-brake equipment for use on severe gradients.

The other 1935 experimental vehicle was no. 32. Its Park Royal body with flowing cream stripes set the standard for the remainder of the pre-war fleet. (Author's collection)

The Conversion Begins

During the years 1937 to 1940, trolleybus wiring was in course of erection along all the remaining tram routes in readiness for each route conversion. The trams often ran using the positive wire of the new overhead, especially away from the town centre and major junctions. Preparations for the new vehicles were sometimes protracted due, for instance, to the need to lower the road under railway bridges on the Birkby and Bradley routes, and for general road reconstruction (eg Paddock on the Longwood route). In such cases temporary motorbus services were operated for some months at a time.

Trolleys Take Over, Route by Route

Trolleybuses were introduced on the ten remaining tram routes, plus one new route, in quick succession. The dates and principal features of each one are given below:

Newsome – service commenced on 2 May 1937, using the eight vehicles previously ordered. This route started in St George's Square, and brought trolleybuses into the main shopping streets of the town, along John William Street and New Street. Instead of turning left at the top of Chapel Hill into East Parade as the Newsome trams had done, the trolleybuses ran down the hill and turned left into Colne Road, regaining the tram route at the junction with Queen Street South. Having climbed the steep Newsome Road, the route was extended from the tram terminus at Newsome Church, and descended Newsome Road South towards Berry Brow. Triangular reversers were provided at both Newsome Church (route no. 21) and the new terminus at Caldercliffe Road (route no. 20), a point designated as Newsome South on destination blinds. On the descent of Newsome Road towards town, the coasting-brake (which limited speed to 15mph) was required to be used between Dawson Road and the bottom of the hill at King's Mill. Details of the eight trolleybuses bought specially for this route are given below:

Nos 33-40 – Park Royal bodies to the streamlined design of no. 32. They had three-leg gantries to the trolley gear on the roof and they were the first Karrier trolleybuses that were not built in the town, production having been moved to Wolverhampton after the takeover of the firm by the Rootes Group.

Crosland Hill – service commenced on 3 October 1937, and again the tram route was extended, further up Blackmoorfoot Road from Crosland Moor to Crosland Hill. Triangular reversers were provided at both points, Crosland Hill being route 60 and Crosland Moor route 61. Like the Newsome route, the vehicles turned at St George's Square in the town centre. On the long descent of Blackmoorfoot Road, the coasting-brake was required to be applied between Frederick Street and the Griffin Inn junction with Manchester Road, although in 1949 the section was shortened to end at Park Road West.

Birkby – service commenced on 7 November 1937. The road under the railway bridge at the town centre end of St John's Road had to be lowered to allow trolleybus operation. The terminus was at Fartown Bar, where a large circle of wiring was installed. It was given route no. 81 (route 80 was proposed to be a new route to Woodhouse via Birkby). The service was linked across the town to the Crosland Hill route, and vehicles from Birkby showed route number '60' or '61' as appropriate, those from Crosland Hill or Crosland

No. 37 is seen in John William Street on the first day of the Newsome trolleybus service. The three-legged trolley gantry is evident on the roof. By this time the Tramways Department had been re-named the Passenger Transport Department and vehicles henceforth showed 'Huddersfield Transport' on their sides rather than 'Huddersfield Tramways'. (W.B. Stocks/ Roy Brook collection)

17

Moor to Birkby showed 81. There was a short-working turning circle at the junction of Birkby Hall Road and Wheathouse Road, this being used for extras catering for workers at the nearby Hopkinson's valve factory. These workings were numbered 82.

Marsden – service commenced on 10 April 1938. In order to turn round, the trolleybuses were extended beyond the tram terminus to Fall Lane, where they turned off the main A62 trunk road. A short-working turning circle was provided at Slaithwaite, and just within the Borough Boundary at Cowlersley there was a 'round the houses' turning loop. The Marsden route number was 40, Slaithwaite and Cowlersley workings being numbered 41 and 43 respectively. A planned reverser at Hoylehouse, situated at the Huddersfield side of Slaithwaite, was never provided, and presumably this point would have been designated route 42. The Marsden trolleybuses were housed in the tram depot at Longroyd Bridge, which was at the time undergoing conversion into a trolleybus depot for the whole fleet. At seven miles, the Marsden route along the Colne Valley had been the longest tram route, and the newest and fastest tramcars delivered in 1931/2 were usually to be found operating it. At this point these trams were offered for sale to other tramway undertakings and were very quickly snapped up by Sunderland Corporation, where they ran for a further sixteen years.

Bradley – service commenced on 19 June 1938. Preparatory work involved increasing the headroom at the Kirkburton branch railway bridge, and the demolition of another nearer the terminus which once carried the Midland Railway branch from Mirfield (closed 1933). Running along Leeds Road, much of which was highly industrialised, the trolleybus route largely matched that of the trams, terminating near the Borough Boundary at the foot of Bradley Lane, where a turning circle was provided at the wide road junction. This terminus was on route no. 40, linked as a through route to

The first trolleybus to Crosland Hill, no 51, is seen here having reversed into Crosland Hill Road at the terminus. This arrangement was replaced in 1950 by a turning circle built on the right of this view. (A.J. Owen)

A typical scene in St George's Square during the tram/trolleybus changeover. Tram no. 108 and trolleybus no. 45 stand together in April 1938. (Roy Brook collection/Paul Watson)

The newest Huddersfield trams, eight English Electric cars built in 1931/2 were taken out of service and sold after the Marsden route trolleybus conversion. No. 144, the highest numbered tram in the fleet, is seen at Marsden terminus shortly before the end of trams on this route. Note that the bamboo pole is raised in readiness to turn the trolley. By this time the automatic trolley reverser, a standard fitment at most tram termini, had been dismantled, the trams using the positive trolleybus wire. (Author's collection)

Marsden. There were several intermediate turning points, these being at Deighton (reverser, route no. 41), British Dyes ('round the houses loop', route no. 42), Canker Lane (turning circle, route no. 43) and at the Huddersfield Town AFC football ground ('round the houses' loop). Route 43 (which also applied to the Cowlersley short-working) was renumbered to 42 during the war to avoid duplication with the motorbus service to Halifax.

A view of Leeds Road at the foot of Whitacre Street, Deighton, shortly before conversion of the Bradley tram route, this point being the rail head at the time. In the background is the Kirkburton branch railway bridge, where the road needed to be lowered to allow trolleybus operation. On the left is a Joint Omnibus Committee bus operating a shuttle service between this point and Bradley tram terminus. Tram 125, using the new trolleybus overhead, sets off on a through service to Dod-Lea, which operated for a short time during this period. To the right is a typical red painted Huddersfield police box. (W.A. Camwell)

Trolleybus no. 42 was the first to operate on the Sheepridge route, and is seen here on Ashbrow Road near the junction with Woodhouse Hill. It will continue via Woodhouse Hill, and being a Sunday morning, will run to Crosland Hill via Birkby (showing route no. 60) using the connecting wires at Fartown Bar. Note the tubular style of overhead suspension, typical of the early wiring installations in the town. This part of Ashbrow Road lost its trolleybus service when the Sheepridge and Woodhouse routes were extended in 1949. (W.B. Stocks/Kirklees Cultural Services)

Sheepridge and Woodhouse – service commenced on 19 June 1938 (concurrent with the Bradley route). The Sheepridge tram terminus had been at the eastern end of Ash Brow Road, at its junction with Woodhouse Hill. The trolleybuses were extended down Woodhouse Hill, then via Fartown Green to rejoin the Sheepridge route at Fartown Bar, thereby forming a circular service in each direction. Woodhouse Hill is very steep, the gradient being 1 in 8½ and special precautions were introduced to ensure safe operation. The use of the coasting brake was compulsory on the descent, and at its narrowest point, trolleybuses were not allowed to pass each other. The Sheepridge route via Smithy was route 10, and the Woodhouse route was route 20, being operated as a through route to Newsome. The original plan to run the Woodhouse route via Birkby as service 80 was never effected.

Longwood – commenced operation on 1 January 1939. This was the Dod-Lea tram route, this name being discontinued for trolleybus operation. This was another route which presented challenges in operation. In Longwood village the

This view shows the remarkable full circle of wiring at Fartown Bar, where all four roads at the junction carried trolleybus routes. The scene looks north along Bradford Road towards Smithy on the Sheepridge route. On the left is Spaines Road leading to the Birkby route, and on the right is Fartown Green Road leading to Woodhouse. This view is dated 12 March 1939, and the separate wiring for the Brighouse trams can be seen cutting through the centre of the circle. (W.E. Turton/Kirkless Cultural Services)

Round she goes! The layout of the turntable at Longwood is shown here in this press photograph shortly after the commencement of the route. (J.P. Senior collection)

these requirements were removed in 1949. The route number was 10, with the intermediate turning circle at Paddock being no. 11, and vehicles ran across the town to Sheepridge. There was another turning point in Longwood village, where a reverser was provided at Prospect Road. However this was rarely used, not least because of its awkward nature – vehicles having to reverse down a steep incline. It was removed in 1944.

Lockwood – operation commenced on 12 January 1939 (peak hours only), and on 20 February 1939 (full service). Lockwood Bar was a regularly used short-working of the Honley tram route. Despite the intention to run trolleybuses to Honley, the Transport Department was beset with difficulties in lowering the headroom of the bridge at the southern end of Lockwood viaduct. Eventually the operation of the route passed to the Joint Omnibus Committee motorbuses, and the trolleybuses ran only as far as a turning circle behind Lockwood Church. This short route was designated no. 50 and there were no intermediate turning points. At this stage the trolleybus fleet was housed entirely at the rebuilt Longroyd Bridge depot, the remaining trams for the West Vale and Brighouse Routes being housed at Great Northern Street.

West Vale – operation commenced on 28 May 1939. This long route reached out to the town of Elland, and beyond. Its main feature was the lengthy climb out of Elland towards Huddersfield known as The Ainleys, and on the descent the coasting-brake was required to be used between the southern-most road bridge at Ainley Top and Sharratt's Brickworks. At West Vale, the trams had reversed in Saddleworth Road, within sight, until 1934, of Halifax trams on their Stainland route. The trolleybuses' 'round the houses' turning loop incorporated Stainland Road where the Halifax trams once ran. The route number was 30, and another 'round the houses' turning point at Elland was route no. 31. At the Borough Boundary at Birchencliffe an unusual reversing triangle was provided, this requiring the vehicle to

roadway was very narrow, and in part of Longwood Gate trolleybuses were prohibited from passing each other. The biggest problem was to find a suitable turning point, and this was solved by the construction of a concrete platform incorporating a turntable, built out from the road at the terminus. There were also two short coasting brake sections – in Vicarage Road near the Quarmby Clough hairpin bend, and in Longwood Road approaching Paddock Head. Both

Stainland Road West Vale is the location of this view of no. 50, possibly on the first day of trolleybus operation. In the left background is no. 135, parked behind the General Manager's car. (Author's collection)

cross the main Halifax Road before reversal into Branch Lane. (Route no. 32).

Brighouse – operation commenced on 30 June 1940. The apparent delay in the final tram to trolleybus conversion was due partly to the outbreak of war, and partly to a wrangle with the LMS railway company regarding the operation of trolleybuses over the bridge at Brighouse Station. Trolleybuses took a slightly longer diversionary route via Bradley Bar between Smithy and Fixby, and the Brighouse terminus was located beyond the former tram terminus, at the north end of the town centre, where a reversing triangle

was provided into Bonegate, beside the Ritz cinema. Route numbers were 90 (Brighouse), 91 (Rastrick – with a triangular reverser at Rastrick Common), and 92 (Bradley Lane – another reverser at Lightridge Road). This route ran to the town centre (St George's Square) only.

The end of the Brighouse trams meant the abandonment of the reserved sleeper track at Fixby. In June 1940, tram no. 109 descends through the fields towards Fartown with passengers enjoying the view from the open balcony. After the rails had been lifted, the track bed remained untouched for well over 20 years, but it has now been largely built over. (R.B. Parr)

Mr Harry Godsmark, General Manager, poses with his wife and Alderman Bennie Gray, Transport Committee chairman, in front of the first trolleybus to Brighouse. The location is Fixby, and the wiring of the Bradley Lane reversing triangle can just be seen to the right of the vehicle. Note the wartime white edging on the vehicle's mudguard. (Travel Lens Photographic)

The Big Vehicle Order – the Pre-war 'Standard' Trolleybuses

In the Autumn of 1936 an order for 85 Karrier trolleybuses was placed. At the time, this was the largest single UK order ever made for trolleybuses. These trolleybuses would be numbered 41 to 125, and all were to a similar specification and appearance to nos 33 to 40. A follow-up order for a further fifteen vehicles was placed in 1938 (nos 126 to 140). These vehicles became the standard pre-war trolleybus for the town. The batches were:

41-105
> Park Royal bodies similar to the 33-40 batch but with two leg trolley gantries which became the norm.

106-115
> Brush bodies, distinguishable by the bright unpainted surrounds to the front windscreens.

116-125
> Weymann bodies with an exaggerated bulbous frontal profile. These vehicles had electro-magnetic contactor equipment which made a sharp clicking sound rather than the electro-pneumatic type of the other 'standards' which operated with slurps and wheezes. For this reason these ten vehicles were nick-named 'Messerschmitts' after the noisy German fighter plane.

126-140
> Park Royal bodies to the previous design, but with slightly lowered windscreens.

Brush bodied no. 112 is seen when brand new, showing the bright metal surrounds to the windscreens which were a distinguishing feature of this batch of vehicle. The location is Manchester Road Slaithwaite, near the Star Hotel. Note the tram track in the left foreground. (A.J. Owen)

The ten Weymann-bodied vehicles, known as 'Messerschmitts', had a more bulbous front end than the other pre-war vehicles. However, the first of the batch, no. 116 is displaying its rear end in this official view taken before delivery. (Author's collection)

Much Ado About Road Reconstruction

Whilst the flurry of work was in progress to convert the tram system to trolleybus operation, there was also much to do to remove the tram rails and reconstruct road carriageways. In three instances this could not be done without causing great disruption to the trolleybus services during the works.

Trinity Street 1937. Between 18 August and 11 October, the Lindley and Outlane routes were diverted away from Trinity Street using newly erected wiring along New North Road to the Blacker Road junction, then turning left along Edgerton Grove Road to rejoin the route at Gledholt. The wiring in New North Road was subsequently retained for use by the West Vale trolleybuses.

Manchester Road 1938-1939. The most prolonged period of disruption took place along Manchester Road, when the tram track was removed from the five-mile section between the Borough Boundary at Spurn Point and Marsden. This work was undertaken from 18 July 1938 to 20 November 1939. Closing the A62 trunk road was impossible, and so the work was done by closing half the width of the carriageway in sections along the route. The original overhead on the route was placed near to the roadside, and therefore operating on the wrong side of the road meant changing the trolleys on to the opposite pair of wires (and then back again) at each section of works. With several sections under repair at the same time, the effect on service reliability can be imagined. Eventually, from December 1938, the through service to Bradley was discontinued and both routes ran separately to and from the town centre in order to limit disruption to the Marsden route. Normal running did not resume until 20 December 1939.

The local press, *The Huddersfield Examiner*, likened the changing of the trolleys to the 'Changing of the Guard', and went on:

"In *addition to the health-giving properties of a trip by 'bus through the Colne Valley, there are certain attractions which make the outing a sheer delight. Chief of these at the moment is watching the conductors of* trolley-buses changing the trolley-arms when it is necessary to cross-over at points where road reconstruction is in progress. This is a real sport, and proving as great an inducement to visit the scene as the bumping and bouncing of the 'buses over the undulating roadway caused by piles of rubbish and fragments of footpaths left thrown about in profusion ... All went well until we reached a point somewhere just beyond Linthwaite ... then we came to a red light and had to stop. There, I was told, the road was open for a short distance for single-line traffic only. I had read the warning boards about 'moving on green only'. But I discovered it was not so easy as all that. You cannot always move on green if you travel by trolley-bus. My interesting friend the conductor began a series of gyrations which made me imagine he had missed his vocation. He ought to have been an acrobat, or something spectacular like that. He, or was it his driver, had seen coming from the opposite direction another stately vehicle with trolley arms disported overhead.

He jumped down from his platform. There followed a rattling noise which startled the occupants of the 'bus and which proved to be the disturbance caused by pulling his (bamboo) trolley pole from its place of refuge at the side of the bus. He whipped it up into the air and there was a titter among the lady passengers as the 'bus was plunged into darkness.

Nearer and nearer came the apparition, which had been the cause of this manoeuvre and there were shouts from the rear of the 'bus of 'come on!, come on!' The approaching trolley-bus and several other vehicles of various descriptions 'came on' and we sat there in darkness watching in sheer wonderment the passage of the pageant.

Then the trolley arm was refixed in the place which gave both light and power. The motorman (sic) who had been to the assistance of his colleague, rushed 'back to the front' if you understand me, climbed into his den, and hastily prepared to restart the vehicle. But the tricky little robot beat him and the tantalising red light appeared. 'Move only on green'. More acrobatics. Trolleys up again, more running this way and that. Can you beat the little red light?"

John William Street, New Street and Buxton Road 1939

These were the town's main shopping streets and a major artery of the trolleybus system. After the conversion of the Lockwood tram route in January 1939, no trams now ran along these streets, and the rails could be removed. This entailed closing the streets to all traffic. All the north to south trolleybus routes had to be diverted via St George's Square, Railway Street, Market Street, Manchester Street, and South Parade to Chapel Hill. Wiring was erected accordingly, and the diversion started on Sunday 2 April. The main loading stops were in Market Street for southbound services and in John William Street (north) for northbound ones. The work was completed by the Summer, and trolleybuses reverted to operating along the main streets on 2 July. A portion of the diversionary wiring (northbound along Market Street) was retained for future use.

A newspaper photograph of Marsden-bound no. 55 on Manchester Road during the period of disruption to the service owing to road works. The conductor is swopping the trolley poles back to the outward wires at the end of a section of single-line working. (J.P. Senior collection)

TROLLEYBUS SERVICES – MAIN ROUTE NETWORK
     AS AT 1 JULY 1940:
(showing through services)
10 Longwood to Sheepridge
20 Newsome to Woodhouse
21 St George's Square to Newsome Church
30 Almondbury to West Vale
33 Almondbury to Market Place
40 Bradley to Marsden
41 Deighton to Slaithwaite
50 Lockwood to St George's Square
60 Birkby to Crosland Hill
61 Birkby to Crosland Moor
71 Waterloo to Lindley
72 Moldgreen to Marsh
73 Waterloo to Outlane
81 Crosland Hill / Crosland Moor to Birkby
90 Brighouse to St George's Square
Note: routes 10 and 20 were linked as through
      journeys at Ashbrow Road (Woodhouse Hill).

The Market Street diversion is depicted here, showing trolleybuses proceeding southbound. No. 45, en route for Crosland Hill is about to pass a temporary queuestand for the Lockwood route. The Ritz cinema is on the extreme left. Note the traction poles are mounted centrally in the carriageway. (W.B. Stocks / Roy Brook collection)

This view of New Street from the Kirkgate junction dates from the late summer of 1939, shortly after the completion of road reconstruction. No. 79 can be seen standing at the Market Place traffic lights. Close examination of this commercial postcard reveals that its conductor is at the front of the upper deck, in process of winding the destination blinds before the vehicle starts a journey to Sheepridge. Thus, showing for only an instant as the final destination is 'Berry Brow', this being a short working of the Honley tram route, but in the event never was a trolleybus destination. (Author's collection)

Another commercial postcard view in New Street, taken at the same period as the previous photograph, shows Brush bodied no. 113 loading at the route 50 Lockwood stop outside Woolworths store. (Author's collection)

5 War, Peace and Post-War Developments

This image, taken from a wartime Karrier Motors advertisement, shows two trolleybuses at Dryclough Road Crosland Moor. Both have probably turned at the short working reverser at this point. No. 90 leading is operating to Birkby, and should be showing route 81 like the following vehicle. The use of this route number ceased in 1940, and vehicles to Birkby then showed no. 61. This is a pre-war photograph doctored to show the wartime white marking paint on the mudguards and the headlight covers. (Author's collection)

After the last trams had run in the first year of the war, Huddersfield's electric public transport was operated by 140 modern vehicles, the oldest of which were seven years old. Unlike some of its near neighbours, the town did not suffer greatly from enemy action, despite there being several engineering 'targets', eg Brook Motors at Longroyd Bridge and David Brown Gears at Crosland Moor.

Tweaks to the Network

There were several changes to the routeings and terminal arrangements during this period, some, not all, being brought about by the wartime situation.

At Fartown, a turning circle was installed on the Woodhouse route at the foot of Woodhouse Hill (shown as Fartown Green on destination blinds) in late 1940. This was probably prompted by operating experience in the previous winter, which was one of the worst on record, and it allowed vehicles to turn whenever the hill was impassable due to snow and ice.

In late 1941, use of the Longwood turntable was discontinued, and a conventional triangular reversing arrangement was installed, vehicles reversing onto the locked turntable platform. This obviated crews having to pull down then re-wire the trolley poles during the blackout. It begs the question why a reverser arrangement was not provided right from the outset.

Spring 1942 saw the linking of the Brighouse and Lockwood routes as a through service, this being route 90,

The post-1943 wiring arrangement at Fartown Bar, which lasted into the 1960s, is depicted here. This view looks from Fartown Green Road across the junction to Spaines Road, where in the distance the Birkby terminal wiring arrangements are just visible. On the extreme left is the wiring connection turning into Spaines Road from the town centre direction which allowed Fartown football specials to operate a one way service – out via Bradford Road and back via Birkby. Coasting across the junction is the first post-war trolleybus, no. 541 whilst operating an enthusiasts' tour in May 1962. (V. Nutton/Travel Lens Photographic)

From 1945, Birkby service trolleybuses used the turning loop erected in 1938 for football specials. This 1960s view shows post-war rebuilt Karrier no. 564 turning from Cobcroft Road into Wasp Nest Road. In the background the wires can be seen emerging from Woodbine Road. At the end of Wasp Nest Road the route turned left back into Spaines Road. Opposite the photographer, out of view on the left, is the author's home up to the age of eleven, and it was watching trolleys making this turn that fired his interest in the subject. 1 February 1964 (Vic Nutton)

and the former Lockwood no. 50 was never used again. Another new feature on the Brighouse route that year was the provision of a turning circle around Bradley Bar round-about. This was designated route 93, although it never saw regular use for another eighteen years.

In 1943 the cumbersome wiring circle at Fartown Bar was removed, this being replaced by a normal wiring junction with no turning facility. Birkby route trolleybuses had therefore to reverse near Fartown Bar at the Spaines Road/Woodbine Road junction, by driving into the latter and reversing out into the former. A 'round the houses' one-way turning loop had been installed here in the autumn of 1938 for use by football specials to the Fartown rugby and cricket ground, and the new Birkby terminal arrangement

therefore used existing wiring at the entry to this loop. This was only short lived, and in July 1945 the Birkby service was extended into the 'round the houses' loop itself with a terminal stop in Woodbine Road.

The final new turning provision before the end of the war in Europe was the erection in March 1945 of a circle at The Griffin junction at Thornton Lodge. Journeys to here showed no. 62.

The New Manager Shows His Colours

In April 1941, a new General Manager took the reins of the Transport Department. Harold Muscroft replaced Harry Godsmark who left to manage the Newcastle Transport undertaking (where he died prematurely in 1946). One of Mr

No. 401 was decorated in a mainly purple livery to celebrate VE day. Seen here in St George's Square, it toured the system but was not operated in public service. (Author's collection)

In 1941, no 75 was given a revised livery style incorporating one shade of red. It was also used to test other experimental features, including sliding windows instead of the standard half-drop type. Renumbered 475 in 1942, it was photographed after the war as seen here. (Author's collection)

Most of the fleet was given the new livery style, including some of the oldest vehicles which previously did not have the cream front below the windscreens. No. 406 displays the new arrangement when seen on football special duty. It is parked on Wasp Nest Road on the storage loop at Fartown in 1945. The building on the right is Fartown Trinity Methodist Church. (A.J. Owen)

From 1941 the oldest trolleybuses numbered 401 to 430 were housed at Great Northern Street, operating only at peak hours. No. 420, one of the 'old tubs', as they were called, is seen about to leave the depot for service in 1945. Note that It does not carry the latest style of livery, retaining a red front, albeit in the lighter shade of red. The doorway arches of the depot, originally rounded, have been squared off to allow use by trolleybuses. (A.J. Owen)

29

Viaduct Street, on to which the Bradford Road trolleybuses were diverted from 1945, goes off to the right of this 1950s view of post-war rebuilt Karrier no. 558. It has come from Birkby and is entering John William Street after emerging from the railway bridge at the end of St John's Road. (Roy Brook/Paul Watson)

Muscroft's first actions was to introduce a new livery style, consisting of a uniform red colour instead of the two shades previously used. The distinctive cream swoop was retained, and 'Huddersfield Corporation' was shown in bold letters along the cream band under the lower-deck windows. The fleet number on the front dash panels was equally bold in black figures and the 'No.' prefix was discontinued. The new design appeared first on trolley no. 75. All but some of the oldest trolleys eventually received this livery. The following year the whole trolleybus fleet was renumbered, having 400 added to their existing number. This was to avoid any confusion with the motorbus fleet, especially during the blackout.

New Routes in the Town Centre

In the latter half of the 1940s, two new route provisions were introduced in the town centre area.

On 21 January 1945, trolleybuses on the Bradford Road routes began to use Viaduct Street in both directions. This street, as its name implies, ran parallel with the railway viaduct leading out of Huddersfield Station towards Leeds, between the north end of John William Street and the Northgate / Bradford Road junction. This relieved pressure in Brook Street in particular, which was often congested due to the proximity of the wholesale vegetable market.

Over two years later a more lengthy diversionary route was introduced, this affecting inward journeys on the Manchester Road routes, which from 9 November 1947 were diverted via Outcote Bank, Manchester Street (adjacent to the Bus Station), Market Street to St George's Square. Part of this routing incorporated wiring previously used for the New Street diversion of 1939. As a result of this change, the cross-town linking of the Longwood route was altered to henceforth operate through to Brighouse as route 90, and the Lockwood route was then linked to Sheepridge as route 10.

The new routing through the town centre introduced in 1947 diverged from Manchester Road, climbing Outcote Bank leading to Manchester Street and Market Street. The steep bank, carrying one-way traffic is seen here, with pre-war rebuilt Karrier no. 498 making the ascent. The roadway was widened for two-way traffic in the mid-1950s. (Roy Brook/Paul Watson)

30

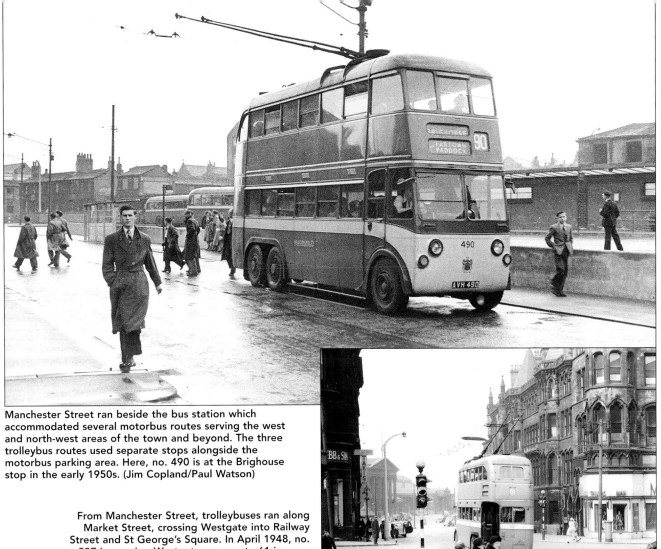

Manchester Street ran beside the bus station which accommodated several motorbus routes serving the west and north-west areas of the town and beyond. The three trolleybus routes used separate stops alongside the motorbus parking area. Here, no. 490 is at the Brighouse stop in the early 1950s. (Jim Copland/Paul Watson)

From Manchester Street, trolleybuses ran along Market Street, crossing Westgate into Railway Street and St George's Square. In April 1948, no. 537 is crossing Westgate on a route 61 journey to Birkby. (Huddersfield Examiner/Trinity Mirror)

This late 1940s view shows no. 535 in Railway Street, entering St George's Square. The site in the background was later occupied by a row of shelters for trolleybus services. Near the end of the decade, the Birkby route was re-numbered from 61 to 60. (Roy Marshall)

Post War Vehicle Developments

The original trolleybus fleet of the early 1930s was, by the mid-1940s, life expired. The Corporation had anticipated this and placed orders during the war for a new fleet of Karrier trolleybuses. By 1947, Karrier chassis were no longer available, and the first batch of eight, nos 541 to 548, which were delivered in July and August, had Sunbeam MS2 chassis, but with Karrier badges. These vehicles were 30 feet long and the Park Royal bodies seated 70 passengers. The body style could be described as 'severe' and the three window arrangement at the front was retained. In the

following year 20 similar vehicles entered service as nos 549 to 568.

Another 24, nos 569 to 592 followed in the first half of 1949, although this latter batch had Sunbeam badges fitted. The new fleet of 52 vehicles replaced many of the earlier pre-war stock. The 'old tubs' as the 401-430 numbered vehicles were known, plus nos 431 to 440 had all disappeared by 1949, as had a few of the earlier 'standard' vehicles, and eight of the Brush bodied batch numbered between 506 and 515, whose bodies were found not to be as sturdy as other types.

Initially, the new trolleys were used almost exclusively on the Bradley to Marsden route. No. 542 is seen at the Marsden stop in John William Street. Behind is one of the 'old tubs', a 1934-built Brush bodied example whose remaining life, in Huddersfield at least, was very short. (A.J. Owen)

The second batch of Karriers MS2s, delivered in 1948, is represented here by no. 565, photographed in Fixby Road. During the 1950s the twin destination apertures over the platform were reduced to one single display. This view was used extensively in Sunbeam promotional literature. (Author's collection)

No.591 was the penultimate Park Royal trolleybus, new in 1949 and part of the later batch. These initially carried the Sunbeam triangular badge under the windscreens as shown, although all lost these subsequently. It is standing at the Lockwood stop in John William Street and is in original condition. (Roy Brook/Paul Watson)

The new northern terminus of route 20 was in the centre of the Riddings housing estate. On the left, no. 580 has just arrived, whilst no. 544 is departing on the right. (Roy Brook/Paul Watson)

Route Extensions in the Northern Hills

The long-awaited expansion of the trolleybus system into council housing areas established to the north of the town shortly before the war came to fruition in 1949. On 6 March of that year the Sheepridge and Woodhouse linked service was broken, and each part was extended separately. Route 10 was run into the Brackenhall estate, terminating at a turning circle at the end of Bradley Boulevard, whilst route 20 now ran to the very top of Woodhouse Hill, then via Chestnut Street and Riddings Road to a turning circle in the estate. The effect of this was that the eastern part of Ash Brow Road, leading to Woodhouse Hill, lost its trolleybus service completely. These route additions took the total route mileage of the system to its maximum extent of 37 miles.

Trolleybus services – the main route network as at 1 January 1950:
(showing through services)
10 Lockwood to Brackenhall
20 Newsome to Riddings
21 St George's Square to Newsome Church
30 Almondbury to West Vale
33 Almondbury to Market Place
40 Bradley to Marsden
41 Deighton to Slaithwate
60 Birkby to Crosland Hill
71 Waterloo to Lindley
72 Moldgreen to Marsh
73 Waterloo to Outlane
90 Brighouse to Longwood

Seen in Westgate at the Waterloo stop in the late 1940s is no. 475, with its experimental sliding windows. This vehicle also survived to be rebuilt. (W.J. Haynes/Paul Watson)

By the end of the 1940s many of the ten Brush bodied Karriers new in 1939 had been withdrawn. This late 1940s scene overlooking the New Street and the Market Place shows no. 508 at the Newsome stop. This vehicle, together with no. 509, survived to be rebuilt with new bodies. (Roy Brook collection/Paul Watson)

6 The 1950s, Losses and Gains

At the end of the 1949, work started to change the layout of St George's Square. This view taken about 1948 shows not only the open area, but also many trolleybuses, either parked in the Square or loading passengers along John William Street – indicative of the high level of service required in the immediate post-war period. (Commercial postcard/Author's collection)

At the dawn of the decade, the Huddersfield trolleybus system was at its peak in terms of route mileage (37), fleet strength (140) and passengers carried (approx 60 million per annum)

Circling the Square

In 1950, big changes were introduced in St George's Square. This was previously a mainly open area where trolleybuses parked in the centre facing John William Street. The new layout consisted of a large central circular flower bed, around which there was a full circle of trolleybus wiring. Spare trolleys were now parked on the west side of this island facing the George Hotel. Later, in the following year, a long passenger shelter was built in Railway Street, and the stops for the Birkby and Brighouse services, which hitherto had their main town centre stands in John William Street alongside the George Hotel, were moved to this new structure from 21 October 1951. Two wiring loops were provided here in the overhead for each service to allow the Bradley route trolleys, whose stop remained alongside the George Hotel, to pass.

This interesting photograph overlooking the Square, taken from Lion Buildings on John William Street is dated 17 December 1949. It shows work in progress to provide a roundabout, new kerbing for this being visible in place on the centre left. Work is also underway on the trolleybus overhead, a new trailing frog assembly being visible in the lower centre, this being for the realigned exit wiring from the Square, which will replace the adjacent frog in due course. (Huddersfield Examiner/Trinity Mirror)

The revised arrangement in St George's Square was completed in the Spring of 1950. The new roundabout is seen in this commercial postcard view. Passing the George Hotel is one of the 1950 Sunbeams, followed by a pre-war Karrier. (Author's collection)

No. 502 pauses beside St George's Square in 1950 to allow passengers to alight before it moves into John William Street to the Birkby stop alongside the George Hotel. (Clarence Carter)

There were three main stops beside the George Hotel, these being for the Brighouse, Bradley and Birkby routes and a wiring loop was provided for these. No. 585 is seen at the Brighouse stop. (Clarence Carter)

This busy 1951 scene looks north along John William Street from St George's Square. It shows trolleybuses at the alighting stop on the right, and also at the stops alongside the George Hotel on the left, where no. 559 can be seen loading passengers for Birkby. No. 548 on the right has the push-out opening window in the middle pane of the upper deck front – these were fitted to all the 1947 and 1948 batches of Karrier MS2s soon after they entered service to improve ventilation. The 1949 Sunbeams were delivered with a sliding window as on the vehicle behind. Also evident on the lower side of no. 548 is the new fleetname 'HuddersfielD', which replaced the 'Huddersfield Corporation' legend on the cream stripe. The Hanson's single-deck AEC bus overtaking the trolleys is arriving in town from Lindley and Weatherhill, on the service which ran parallel with the Birkby trolleys along St John's Road as far as Blacker Road. (John Fozard)

An early 1950s portrait of no. 522, one of the ten Weymann-bodied vehicles known as 'Messerschitts'. Six of these were rebuilt with new Roe bodies, but this one remained unaltered until final withdrawal in 1955. Its bulbous front panels are evident in this view taken at John William Street. (Roy Brook/Paul Watson)

Rebuilds (1) – The Pre-War Karriers

Although some of the earliest trolley-buses had been withdrawn from service by 1950, the majority of the pre-war fleet was still around and badly in need of overhaul. To extend their lives, twenty-eight of these were given a full chassis rebuild, their Park Royal bodies scrapped and new bodies fitted by C.H. Roe of Leeds. They were dealt with in four batches of seven between 1950 and 1954. (This was not the first instance of a Huddersfield trolley receiving a new body – no. 28 was destroyed by fire in thick fog in 1940, a consequence of prolonged running on low notches of power. It was given a new Park Royal body of the streamlined style of later vehicles, but was withdrawn in 1948). It was intended that Roe would provide body shells only, with the Transport Department fitting out the vehicles themselves. The first seven vehicles were so treated, but the remainder were built as complete bodies by Roe. No. 493 was the first, entering service in August 1950, and the batch was complete by early 1954 when no. 524 appeared. These, and all subsequent rebodied vehicles, were always referred to as 'rebuilds'.

The Fleet Changes Shape

The new Roe bodies on the rebuilds introduced modern, sleek looking vehicles. Gone were the angular lines and 'three window front' arrangement of the earlier post-war trolleys. The design incorporated a new destination arrangement, whereby the terminus and 'via' points were combined in one display. Another innovation was the provision of stout, and very heavy, front and rear bumpers. The intention of these was that the vehicles could push each other in emergencies and park closer together in the depot.

The first rebuild was no. 493 in August 1950. The modern lines of the new bodywork are evident in this scene in New Street shortly after the vehicle entered service. (Clarence Carter)

This photograph was taken on the same day and location as the previous one, allowing a comparison between rebuilt and un-rebuilt vehicles. No. 537 is on a journey to Riddings, but still displays the defunct destination 'Woodhouse'. (Clarence Carter)

Among the first batch of rebuilds were two of the former Brush bodied vehicles. One of these, no. 509, is seen in John William Street in the early 1950s. (Roy Brook/Paul Watson)

The later pre-war rebuilds had sliding cab doors, as shown by no. 540 standing at Outlane terminus. (Author's collection)

The new Roe-bodied Sunbeam MS2's delivered in 1950/1 were particularly handsome vehicles. It was common practice for official views such as this to be taken in Fixby Road, and no. 600 is showing the correct destination and route number for the Fixby short-working of the Brighouse route. (Author' collection)

The second batch of BUT trolleybuses entered service in 1956. Brand new no. 626 is seen loading at the Fixby stop (formerly Brighouse) in Railway Street adjacent to St George's Square. (Author's collection)

In 1953 the first batch of BUT trolleybuses arrived, this official view showing the rear aspect of the East Lancashire bodywork. By this time the Fixby short-workings had been re-numbered to 91 as shown here. (Author's collection)

Delivered almost concurrently with the first batch of rebuilds were fourteen brand new trolleys – these being the Sunbeam MS2 type with Roe bodies to the same design, but slightly longer seating 70 passengers instead of 66. These vehicles were numbered 593 to 606. No. 593 was exhibited at the Commercial Motor Show in London in November 1950, and for this event it was given gold lining, red bumpers and wheels (instead of the normal black), chromium plated fittings and light coloured leather facings to the moquette seating. This batch of vehicles was the first not to have regenerative braking on the power pedal, and they had automatic acceleration equipment which prevented the driver 'notching up' too quickly.

Arriving at the latter end of 1953 were twelve more new trolleys, and again these brought new features to the fleet. Nos 607 to 618 had British United Traction (BUT) chassis with East Lancashire Coachbuilders bodywork to the general modern design of the previous Roe bodies. Their motors were rated at 150hp – the most powerful in the fleet. A further twelve vehicles of the same type followed in 1956, these being numbered 619 to 630.

To celebrate the Queen's Coronation in June 1953, no. 535 was decorated in a patriotic red white and blue livery. It operated in normal passenger service during the period, and immediately afterwards it was withdrawn for rebuilding with a new Roe body. In the left background of this scene in John William Street is the similarly decorated Transport Offices. (Roy Brook/Paul Watson)

The Brighouse terminus was off Bradford Road at Bonegate. No. 553 has reversed into the latter road on 28 July 1951. Until 1931, a single-track Halifax Corporation tramway ran along here to Halifax via Hipperholme, and traces of this can still be seen in the roadway. (Jim Copland/Paul Watson)

Brighouse No More

In the early 1950s, the costs of operating trolleybuses on the Brighouse route were causing concern. The situation in 1952 was that the frequency of service 90 to Brighouse was every 20 minutes, being augmented during the day by a journey to Fixby only (the post-war designation of the Bradley Lane turning point) which gave a 10-minute frequency to this point. These Fixby workings had been renumbered from 92 to 91 in that year.

Between Fixby and Brighouse the trolleybus service was largely paralleled by two Joint Omnibus Committee motorbus services, both running hourly, one via Cowcliffe and the other via Fartown and Netheroyd Hill. By 1955 it was decided to curtail the trolleybuses at Fixby (the Borough boundary), and also one of the motorbus services at Cowcliffe, leaving the other motorbus service to operate every 20 minutes via a slightly altered route into Brighouse. The Brighouse trolleybuses last ran on Saturday 9 July 1955, and thereafter Fixby became the terminus of the shortened route 90.

This is the main stop in Brighouse town centre, which was the former tram terminus for Huddersfield. (Jim Copland/Paul Watson)

At Brighouse Station, the route turned off the main Huddersfield Road into Gooder Lane towards Rastrick. (Roy Brook/Paul Watson)

Following the Brighouse route closure, the remainder of the distinctive unrebuilt pre-war 'Messershmitt' trolleys were withdrawn. No. 523 (which was rebuilt and ran until 1963), is seen in its original form heading a line-up in Ashgrove Road on the ICI turning loop, Leeds Road. (W.J. Haynes/Paul Watson)

The first rebuilds of post-war vehicles entered service in the Spring of 1955, in time to be photographed on the Brighouse route. No. 557 is seen in New Hey Road Rastrick on the last day of trolleybus operation on the route. It is about to make the sharp left turn into Clough Lane at the Sun Inn. (Roy Brook/Paul Watson)

Rebuilds (2) – Post-war Karrier / Sunbeams

The success of the pre-war rebuilds led the Transport Department to adopt this practice between 1955 and 1959 for many of the 52 post-war Karrier / Sunbeam MS2 type vehicles. Eighteen of these chassis (in three batches of six) received new East Lancashire bodies to the similar design of those mounted on the new BUT vehicles, between 1955 and 1957. A further fifteen vehicles received new Roe bodies (in three batches of five) between 1958 and 1960. These latter vehicles were an updated design of the previous Roe bodies, dispensing with interior wood-work and incorporating fibreglass roof domes. By the end of the 1950s, only nineteen vehicles retained their original Park Royal bodies.

This typical Huddersfield street scene shows Bridge Street, Lockwood on a wet day in September 1954. Karrier no. 561, having just started its journey from the terminus, is picking up passengers on the bridge over the River Holme. On the right is a red police box and on the left skyline is Newsome. This vehicle was rebuilt in 1956 with a new East Lancashire body. (Jim Copland/Paul Watson)

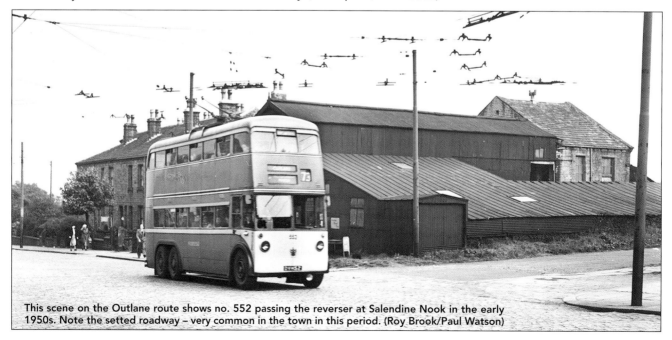

This scene on the Outlane route shows no. 552 passing the reverser at Salendine Nook in the early 1950s. Note the setted roadway – very common in the town in this period. (Roy Brook/Paul Watson)

No 552 is seen again, this time in rebuilt form. It is standing at the
Fixby terminus of route 90. The reverser is in the left background,
and the former Brighouse route continued into the left distance.
(Jim Copland/Paul Watson)

This wintry scene shows the main Almondbury stop in Byram Street,
with St Peter's Parish Church in the background. Upon departure, no.
557 will turn immediately to the left of this view into St Peter's Street.
(Roy Brook/Paul Watson)

A view looking north along John William Street showing no. 556 at the Longwood stop, which until the early 1960s was outside the YMCA building. This was demolished and new YMCA premises were erected in Lord Street. In the left background no. 630 waits at the stops for the Brackenhall and Riddings routes. (Roy Brook/Paul Watson)

The final batch of 1950s rebuilds with East Lancashire bodies, entering service in 1957, had slightly shorter dash panels under the windscreen, like the 1956 BUTs. No. 566 is in Colne Road on the Newsome route, having just turned sharply through a 90-degree corner from King's Mill bridge. This was a highly industrialised area of mills and engineering works. (Peter Mitchell)

Representing the type of Roe body placed on post-war rebuilt MS2 chassis is no. 571. It is at the top of Wheathouse Road on the Birkby route, near the junction with Birkby Hall Road. Here there was a short working turn-round loop in the wide junction, situated in the left background of this view. This was designated route no. 62, for special journeys serving the nearby Hopkinson's valve works and there was a siding further down Wheathouse Road for specials to wait clear of the service trolley wiring. The destination blind has not been changed and should be showing 'Crosland Hill'. (Peter Mitchell)

The terminus of the extended Bradley route was at the junction of Keldregate and Bradley Lane. Here, no. 581 departs on a journey to Marsden, almost twelve miles distant. (Peter Mitchell)

Into Keldregate

Within a year, the loss of the Brighouse trolleybus route was partly recompensed by the opening on 2 April 1956 of a spur off the Bradley route, into the Keldregate housing area. This branched off the existing route about a third of a mile before the terminus, running along Brooklands and Keldregate to terminate at the junction with Bradley Lane, where a turning circle was provided. This extension, of just under ½ mile in length, became no. 40, and the old terminus, became known as Bradley (Leeds Road), took the number 41, the service running through to Slaithwaite. Some overhead fittings and traction poles recovered from the Brighouse route were used for this project.

Originally designated route 40, the Bradley Leeds Road terminus was renumbered to 41 when the Keldregate extension opened. Seen at the terminal stop is no. 608. Note in the background traction pole repainting is under progress, the contractor's vehicle being used to put the final green coat of paint over the silver undercoat. (Peter Mitchell)

The town centre terminus of the Leeds Road football special trolleys was at the north end of Byram Street. Here, on 20 August 1955, no. 477 has just unloaded football fans returning from the match, and is about to return to the ground for another load. Note the 'fare 3d' sign on the route number blind – this assisted away fans and also conductors, who had to collect 60-plus fares during a ride taking only a few minutes. (Jim Copland/Paul Watson)

School Transport

In 1957, a campus of three schools was built at Salendine Nook, two of which, Huddersfield New College and Huddersfield Girls' High School, would accommodate pupils from all over the town. An anticlockwise loop of wiring was erected within the grounds to cater for the many school special workings. Although opened for use by trolleys in the Spring of 1958, power supply problems initially limited their use, and it was not until a substation was built that sufficient power was available to allow a full requirement of trolleybus specials to operate. By Autumn 1960, there were up to sixteen school specials operating morning and afternoon, the former being through journeys from outside termini. – (see photographs on pages 171-173)

Football Specials

There were two football grounds to which trolleybuses regularly operated special journeys for fans.

Huddersfield Town ground, Leeds Road

This was the home of Huddersfield Town AFC, which, until the 1950s was a successful First Division team. Trolleys operated a shuttle service from the north end of Byram Street to the ground, where there were two turning loops, one around Bradley Mills Lane/Bradley Mills Road, and the other at Canker Lane. Towards the end of the 1950s, when the team was relegated into the Second Division, the Canker Lane loop was sufficient to accommodate the specials and the Bradley Mills loop fell out of use.

Trolleys working football specials were parked in the Canker Lane turning area when the match was in progress. Vehicles were shoe-horned into the space as can be seen in this view. After the match, the vehicles pulled across Leeds Road in turn to load the homeward bound fans. Nos. 586 and 584 head the pack in this view taken about 1960. Both vehicles would be rebuilt in 1963 and 1962 respectively. (Roy Marshall)

No. 542 is seen pulling out of the Canker Lane circle on to Leeds Road (avoiding a near miss with the Ford Zodiac car) after dropping Football fans at the ground. It will return to the town centre (Byram Street) to pick up another load. (Vic Nutton/Travel Lens photographic)

On the other side of Leeds Road a loop of wiring was provided along Bradley Mills Lane and Bradley Mills Road, which ran alongside the east side of the ground. After the team's fortunes waned in the mid-1950s and attendances dropped, this loop was not normally used, all football specials being accommodated in the Canker Lane circle. The wiring remained until April 1965, and no. 590 is seen alongside the ground on Bradley Mills Road during an enthusiasts' tour in March 1963. (Vic Nutton/Travel Lens Photographic)

Huddersfield Rugby League and Cricket ground, Spaines Road

The Fartown ground, situated near the Birkby terminus, was the home of Huddersfield's Rugby League club and its main cricket club. Specials operated to and from the ground via a one-way circuit from Brook Street, out via Northgate and Bradford Road to Fartown Bar, returning via the Birkby route to town. Until 1945, vehicles were stored in the specially provided loop off Spaines Road, as well as Spaines Road itself. Later, after the Birkby service terminus was transferred into this loop, Spaines Road became the main storage area.

Specials from the rugby ground at Fartown returned to town via Birkby. In 1949, a curve was erected outside the Empire cinema in John William Street to allow these workings to turn directly into Brook Street, where they loaded/unloaded. No. 529 is seen using this curve, fans alighting from the vehicle as it waits for the conductor to re-board after pulling the trigger. (Roy Brook/Paul Watson)

Specials parked in Spaines Road, Fartown awaiting the end of a sports event at the Fartown Ground. Visible in this early post-war view is no. 448. (A.J. Owen)

A New Manager – and Plans for Expansion

Harold Muscroft, the Transport Department General Manager since 1941 retired in April 1958, having overseen the post-war development of the trolleybus system. His post was taken by Edgar Dyson, who was locally born. As was usual when a new boss took the helm, there were changes in outlook, and the appearance of the trolley fleet was changed when the black wheels were painted red, and the cumbersome bumpers, which never really achieved their intended purpose, began to be removed from the vehicles, chiefly at overhaul stage. The last quintet of Roe rebuilds on MS2 chassis which entered service from late 1959 were delivered without them.

Even before Mr Muscroft left, a ½-mile extension to the Riddings route was approved, which would take the route into the Deighton housing estate, terminating at a turning circle just ½-mile from the Keldregate terminus. Preparatory work soon commenced, and the line of route even appeared in the Transport Department's map in the timetable booklet. Further extensions were proposed, these being a spur off the Crosland Hill route along Balmoral Avenue to a reverser at Sutherland Drive, and an extension of the Moldgreen trolley route along Long Lane to Dalton, terminating at the Black Horse public house.

The second and final type of Roe bodies is seen here on no. 581 at the Byram Street stop of the Almondbury route. These vehicles were delivered without bumpers and there was an additional emergency exit situated in the first window of the lower deck behind the driver's cab. (John Fozard)

One of the post-war vehicles that were not rebuilt until the 1960s is seen here near the end of its life with its original body. Having come along Leeds Road from the terminus, no. 546 is approaching the junction with Brooklands on a journey to Cowlersley. (Peter Mitchell)

The Last Six-wheelers

The final months of the 1950s saw the entry into service of ten new trolleybuses. These reverted to the Sunbeam make, being of the S7 type. The bodies, by East Lancashire Coachbuilders, had interiors in modern plastic materials of a dark pink colour. Numbered 631 to 640, they were the last wholly new trolleybuses built for the town. Although the legal maximum dimensions for two-axle bus chassis had been increased over the last 12 years to 30 feet in length and 8 feet in width, Huddersfield chose to retain the three-axle layout with narrow bodies. Therefore these vehicles were the last six-wheel trolleybuses built for British use. They were not as sturdy as the previous BUT trolleys, having a pronounced transmission groan when travelling at speed, and some subsequently spent periods off the road awaiting spares. Their introduction allowed withdrawal of the last two unrebuilt pre-war trolleys, nos 476 and 531. This duo, reminders of a past age, had soldiered on working peak-hour specials since the withdrawal of their remaining sisters in 1956. Also taken out of service were eight of the pre-war rebuilds.

The official view taken of 1959 Sunbeam S7 no. 637 in Fixby Road. In the background is the entrance to the Huddersfield Crematorium, opened in 1958. (Author's collection)

The arrival of the new Sunbeams resulted in the withdrawal of the last two unrebuilt pre-war Karriers, nos 476 and 531. Latterly they were used on peak hour specials and football workings. Both are seen here in John William Street at the Bradley stop, making their way from the depot to Byram Street (via Brook Street, Northgate and Northumberland Street). (John Fozard)

The new vehicles also caused the withdrawal of some of the rebuilt pre-war Karriers. These included no. 475, the lowest numbered of the rebuilds. On 23 April 1957 it is seen parked in the lower half of St George's Square. (Jim Copland/Paul Watson)

7 The 1960s, Boom to Bust

A Promising Future?

For the Huddersfield trolleys, the 1960s started out full of promise. The 120-strong fleet included ten brand new vehicles, and 53 older vehicles had received new bodies since 1950. Three new route extensions were actively planned, and the travelling public had every expectation that 'their' trolleys would be around for years to come. However, only three months into this decade came the first cloud of doom. The Transport Committee considered, and approved, a proposal to convert the trolley routes that ran beyond the Borough Boundary (ie West Vale and Marsden) plus the low-frequency Fixby route (by now reduced to running every 30 minutes), to motorbus operation. The Manager was also instructed to prepare a report on the possible conversion of the whole trolleybus system. Not surprisingly, the public reaction was negative to these developments, but the Corporation pressed ahead and orders for new motorbuses (to be wholly Corporation-owned) were placed in the summer of 1960 to run on the West Vale and Marsden routes. In the event, the Fixby trolleybus route was temporarily spared because the Corporation did not wish to hand over this operation, wholly within the Borough, to the Joint Omnibus Committee as originally planned.

Consideration about the future of the whole trolleybus system dragged on until October 1962, when the Town Council finally decided, by a majority of one vote, to gradually replace the remaining trolleybuses with motorbuses. At this stage it was envisaged that this process would take until the early 1970s, by which time the newest trolleys would be life- expired.

Major Road Works

For much of the 1960s, there was considerable upheaval on the roads around the town centre, due to the development of the Inner Ring Road and the new Civic Centre. Despite unwelcome political manoeuvrings regarding the future of the trolleys, their limited time left in service was marked by more tangible manoeuvrings through road works and areas resembling building sites.

The works, converting existing roads into dual carriageway, covered the following areas:

Northgate (junction with Fitzwilliam Street) southwards along Southgate to Shore Head (1960-63)

Leeds Road (junction with Fitzwilliam Street) extended to meet Northgate at the foot of Northumberland Street (1960)

Shore Head to Wakefield Road (just beyond the Somerset Road junction) (1961-1967)

Chapel Hill (1961)

New Hey Road Oakes Bay Horse to Crosland Road (1965-66)

New roundabouts were constructed at Chapel Hill (top), Shore Head and Northumberland Street / Northgate.

Before the road reconstruction of late 1960, Northumberland Street ran direct from Leeds Road, and crossed Northgate halfway along its length. where no. 583 is seen. The new roundabout was built here. The open area in the background is a consequence of demolition of old housing. Note the tank on a road transporter parked in the right background. (Peter Mitchell)

Southgate was widened, and a roundabout constructed at Shore Head in 1962/3. From then, trolleybuses leaving the town centre to Almondbury or Waterloo were diverted onto Oldgate because they were unable to cross on to the new carriageway from Kirkgate. Prior to these changes, no. 554 is seen on Southgate approaching Shore Head. (Roy Brook/Paul Watson)

The portion of Wakefield Road converted into a dual-carriageway formation included two bridges. No. 595 is crossing the Huddersfield Narrow Canal at Aspley. Further east was Somerset Bridge over the River Colne. (Robert Mack)

Chapel Hill was rebuilt in 1961, the carriageway being widened as far as the Colne Road junction. This view, dating from about 1957, shows no. 581 climbing towards the town centre on a through journey to Brackenhall. The prominent building under process of demolition is the municipal 'Model Lodging House'. (Roy Brook / Paul Watson)

In winter, the Outlane route was often subject to snowy weather. This 1950s scene shows New Hey Road, Oakes, with no. 553 climbing towards Outlane. In the mid-1960s, this part of the road was widened to dual-carriageway, and the property on the right, including the chimney of Oakes Mill, was demolished. Shortly after new wiring had been erected over the new westbound carriageway in March 1966, the replacement metal mill chimney partially collapsed in high winds, damaging the overhead fittings. (Roy Brook/Paul Watson)

This is the wiring junction at the top of Chapel Hill before the changes wrought by the Inner Ring Road development. No. 634, almost brand new, takes the Manchester Road wires on a journey to Marsden. The wires on the right lead down Chapel Hill for the Newsome and Lockwood trolleys. (Travel Lens Photographic)

Rebuilds (3) –
Post-War Karrier / Sunbeams of the 1960s

Despite the uncertainty surrounding the trolleybus system, the vehicle rebuilding programme resumed in 1961. East Lancashire Coachbuilders secured a contract to build twelve new bodies on rebuilt chassis. Four entered service in the Spring of 1961, and a further four in 1962. These bodies were very similar to those supplied on the 1959 Sunbeams. The order for the final quartet was altered to six motorbus bodies, but the four trolleybus chassis, already overhauled, eventually received East Lancashire bodies built in the mid-1950s and transferred from slightly older chassis. These entered service during 1963, no. 592 being the last in October of that year. Of the 52 trolleybuses new in the 1940s, only seven now retained their original Park Royal bodywork.

Work is underway to realign the overhead in this view at the top of the widened Chapel Hill. In the background is the wiring junction with the Manchester Road routes (going off to the left), where the new roundabout is being installed. No. 547 is at a temporary stop, opposite derrick no. A7. (Vic Nutton/Travel Lens Photographic)

This scene at Longroyd Bridge shows no. 585, still with its original Park Royal body, opposite Longroyd Bridge depot, with the Paddock viaduct in the background. Note that 'via Keldregate' is being displayed, this being added to some 'via' blinds after 1956 when the Keldregate extension opened. 25 May 1961. (Tony Belton)

In the Spring of 1962, 585 re-entered service with a new East Lancashire body, this being the last trolleybus body built on a six-wheel trolleybus chassis for British service. Here it is at the top of Northumberland Street on route 40 to Marsden. (Vic Nutton/Travel LensPhotographic)

Motorbuses for West Vale, Marsden and Other Areas

In the midst of all these other developments, the planned substitution of trolleybuses for motorbuses had taken place.

The West Vale route trolleybuses last ran on 8 November 1961, after which eight new Leyland motorbuses commenced operation (these being advertised by the Transport Department as 'diesel buses' as if this was some kind of new invention!). The new service terminated at St George's Square using the vacant stand in between the Birkby and Fixby trolleybus stops. The Almondbury trolley-

buses then ran a shuttle service to and from Byram Street as route 33. Surprisingly, no trolleybuses were withdrawn at this time, although eight vehicles (two 1950 Sunbeams and six BUTs) were delicensed and placed in store in Longroyd Bridge depot until November 1962, when eight of the remaining rebuilt pre-war Karriers were withdrawn for scrapping.

The town centre stop for the West Vale route was in Westgate, just above the New Street crossing and outside the Wellington Hotel. A loop was provided to allow Lindley and Outlane trolleys to pass. No. 640, seen here, is about to set off on a short working journey to Birchencliffe. (Clarence Carter)

Trolleys turned at West Vale by means of a one-way loop. No. 577 has just set down passengers in Saddleworth Road, and is about to turn into Stainland Road to reach the terminal stop. (Roy Brook / Paul Watson)

Between West Vale and Elland, trolleybuses ran along Long Wall. This road clung to the hillside at Hullen Edge, giving views across the valley. Nos 632 and 618 can be seen passing here. (Vic Nutton/Travel Lens Photographic)

On reaching Ainley Top, at the summit of the climb from Elland towards Huddersfield, the route passed under two bridges. Here, no. 543 is seen, before it descends through Birchencliffe towards town. Note that tubular suspension was retained at these bridges, the second one of which is visible in the background. (Vic Nutton/Travel Lens Photographic)

At the Blacker Road junction in Edgerton, Halifax Road runs into New North Road. Negotiating the traffic lights and roadworks is no. 574, crossing into Halifax Road. To the left Blacker Road descends to Birkby, and on the right Edgerton Grove Road climbs to Gledholt on the Lindley/Outlane route, this road being temporarily wired for trolleybuses in 1937. (Vic Nutton/Travel Lens Photographic)

This introduction of Corporation motorbuses inevitably meant that the planned trolleybus route extensions were introduced as motorbus routes. The first of these was the Deighton via Riddings route (no. 22) which commenced on 1 March 1962. Operated by one vehicle, it ran to and from the town centre, shadowing the Riddings trolleybuses. It became the first motorbus service to invade the main shopping area of the town, using the Riddings trolleybus stop in John William Street. The services to Crosland Hill (Balmoral Avenue – no. 61) and Dalton (Black Horse – no. 70) were introduced later in 1962 and these also largely shadowed trolleybus routes.

No. 493, the original rebuilt pre-war Karrier survived in service until the end of October 1962. It is seen here in March 1962 at Fartown Bar, operating an enthusiast's tour for the Doncaster Omnibus and Light Railway Society. Standing behind it is one of the inaugural batch of Corporation owned motorbuses bought to replace trolleybuses on the West Vale route, painted in the so-called 'trolleybus style' livery. It is working on route 22, which ran to Deighton via Riddings, originally planned to be a trolleybus operated extension of route no. 20. (John Fozard)

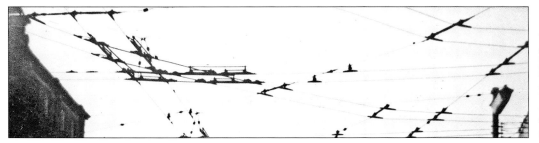

The overhead wiring crossing assembly at the junction of Railway Street and Westgate, erected in 1962, is seen here in detail, looking from Railway Street towards Market Street. (Philip Jenkinson)

55

Looking towards the overhead wiring junctions above Westgate and Market Street, no. 575 is seen loading at the Birkby stop in Railway Street. The wiring loop for this is evident. In the background can be seen two trolleys (the rearmost being no. 624) about to turn into Westgate to commence service. Approaching is a trolleybus-replacement West Vale motorbus, whose stop was at the centre part of the Railway Street shelter. (Vic Nutton/Travel Lens Photographic)

This view looks up Westgate, showing the junction with Market Street and the main Waterloo / Moldgreen stops on the left. The driver of no. 614 hauls himself into the cab. Note the loop for these services, the passing wires being used by trolleys from West Vale on their way to the Almondbury stop in Byram Street. (Vic Nutton/Travel Lens Photographic)

Seen at the top of Westgate, near the junction of Trinity Street and New North Road is no. 561 on its way down Westgate in 1962. It is passing the Brockholes motor showroom (a Ford dealer) and Whiteley's Café. Note the convertible Triumph Herald. This view dates from after the demise of the West Vale trolleybus route, which ran up New North Road in the background. Also of note is the trailing frog of the wiring link from Market Street, erected in 1960. The body on this trolley was transferred to no. 591 in 1963. (John Fozard)

It was over a year before the long Marsden route succumbed to motorbuses, this occurring during the 'big freeze' of January 1963, the last trolleybus running on the 30th. The effect of the Marsden conversion on other trolleybus routes was quite dramatic, as will be described shortly. At this point all the existing pre-war Karriers were withdrawn, together with eight post-war vehicles, all rebuilds that would have been due for overhaul. It was the bodies of four of these latter vehicles that were transferred to later chassis as mentioned above.

No. 563 is seen turning at the small roundabout at the Marsden terminus, Fall Lane. (Peter Mitchell)

The seven-mile Marsden route was largely on the A62 trunk road along the Colne Valley. At Linfit Steps, near Slaithwaite is no. 584, which is about to pull up at the stop. This vehicle was subsequently rebuilt in 1962. (Peter Mitchell)

The Marsden and Crosland Hill routes diverged at the 'Griffin' junction at Thornton Lodge. In the mid-1950s, no. 564 has operated the automatic frog to take the wires along Manchester Road. The re-setting skate can be seen just after the frog assembly. The railway bridge carries the railway to Penistone. (Roy Brook/Paul Watson)

The route crossed into the Borough of Huddersfield near Cowlersley. There was a short-working loop here, which ran around New Street and Pickford Street (route no. 42). In the snow of early 1963, no. 561 turns from New Street into Pickford Street. Note the semaphore direction indicator in use. On the left is the wall of the New Street Council School. (Vic Nutton/Travel Lens Photographic)

The Trolleybus Routes Shake-up of 1963

The Marsden conversion in January 1963 resulted in a reorganisation of some of the remaining routes. The Bradley route was linked to Longwood as route 40, this being quite straightforward. This left the Fixby route unattached to a cross-town partner, and it was decided to link this route to the other existing 'orphan', the Almondbury route. This was far from simple. To allow Fixby trolleybuses access to the Byram Street area, the stretch of wiring in Northgate, from Bradford Road to the foot of Brook Street, which had not been used in public service since 1945 (apart from Fartown football specials in the northbound direction only), was brought back into use. Additionally, entirely new wiring was erected in the southbound direction along Lord Street from Northumberland Street to Kirkgate. The town centre Almondbury stop was to be moved to Lord Street, and the wiring in the lower part of St Peter's Street, turning right onto Southgate was abandoned, owing to the dual carriageway being built in this location. The existing Almondbury stop in Byram Street became the Fixby stop (moving from the Railway Street shelter), and again new wiring was erected eastbound down Northumberland Street onto Northgate. The new arrangements came into force on 31 January 1963, and the Fixby to Almondbury route was numbered 34.

Derrick A10 is at work in the freezing conditions of January 1963 erecting the overhead in Lord Street in readiness for the introduction of trolleybuses along here at the end of the month. This 1958-built AEC Mandator was converted into a towing wagon in the following year, losing its tower in the process. (Vic Nutton/Travel Lens Photographic)

Part of the Lord Street wiring came into use on 24 January 1963, a few days before the new route started. This view shows no. 615 turning from St Peter's Street into Lord Street on that day. It was still using the original Almondbury stop in Byram Street, and previously its route would have been straight along St Peter's Street to Southgate, as per the motorbus in the background. The wiring link from Northumberland Street has yet to be completed. Note the atrocious road conditions, and the Guy motorbus of County Motors on the left. (Vic Nutton/Travel Lens photographic)

From Northumberland Street the re-routed trolleys from Fixby turned left into Lord Street. With Northumberland Street in the background, no. 593 passes a Hebble AEC motorbus, which is working on the Bradford route, jointly worked with Huddersfield JOC and Bradford Corporation. 29 May 1965. (Author)

After leaving Byram Street, Fixby trolleys ran down Northumberland Street to Northgate, using new wiring. No. 609 having just departed from the Byram Street stop, takes the new wires as it prepares to turn right into Northumberland Street. In the background is Huddersfield Parish Church, and a Hanson's single deck AEC bus on the Lindley Moor/Weatherhill service. (David Beach)

No. 586 entered service with the body from no. 556 in the Spring of 1963. It is seen at the Riddings stop in John William Street. (John Fozard)

During 1963, four of the remaining un-rebuilt post-war Park royal vehicles received East Lancashire bodies taken from trolleybuses withdrawn in 1962/3. One of these was no. 592, seen here in original condition at Outlane in the 1950s. It re-entered service carrying the body from no. 563 in October 1963. (Roy Brook/Paul Watson)

Trolleybus services – the main route network as at 31 January 1963: (showing through services)	
10 Lockwood to Brackenhall	34 Almondbury to Fixby
20 Newsome to Riddings	40 Bradley Keldregate to Longwood
21 St George's Square to Newsome Church	41 Bradley Leeds Road to Slaithwaite
33 Almondbury to Market Place	60 Birkby to Crosland Hill
	71 Waterloo to Lindley
	72 Moldgreen to Marsh
	73 Waterloo to Outlane

Another of the vehicles that received a pre-used body was no. 587, which was given the body from no. 557. It is seen between Quarmby Clough and Paddock, which was one of the last places on the system that trolleys ran on stone sett paving. Note Nab End tower on the hilltop in the distance, and Longwood village in the left background. (Roy Brook / Paul Watson)

Towards the end of May 1963, a Civics Exhibition was held at the Town Hall. For this a Leyland motorbus owned by Yorkshire Woollen District Transport, which had been converted to resemble an open-top tram to celebrate their 50th anniversary, was hired to transport local schoolchildren visiting the event. It is parked in St George's Square, about to be overtaken by no. 588 which is working on the no. 21 Newsome Church service. (Roy Brook)

At the old Crosland Moor tram terminus there was a reverser into Dryclough Road (designated route no. 61), but after 1957 trolleys seldom turned here. This view at Dryclough Road shows the reverser wires on the left. No. 619, ascending to the Crosland Hill terminus is being passed by no. 604. Note the corner shops and the red police box on the left. (Vic Nutton/Travel Lens Photographic)

The notable feature of the Birkby route was the veritable roller-coaster ride known as the 'Birkby switchback', consisting of two opposing steep gradients in succession along Birkby Hall Road. No. 590 is seen at the Halifax Old Road junction having traversed the 'switchback' which is in the background. On the right, beside Norman Park, is one of the shelters erected in the early years of the 20th century for tram passengers. This example was dismantled in the 1970s and re-erected at the Trolleybus Museum at Sandtoft. (Vic Nutton/Travel Lens Photographic)

This wintry 1950s scene on the Crosland Hill route is at Park Road West, where the coasting brake section ended. No 571 is seen on the descent towards Manchester Road. (Roy Brook/Paul Watson)

A scene in St John's Road Birkby, at the Blacker Road junction. Here no. 541 has come from the town, and passengers are alighting at this very busy stop. Through the trees above the pillar box can be seen the 'Trolley Bus Stop' plate which is mounted on a separate post. Most Huddersfield trolleybus stops where shelters were not provided were painted on a traction pole. (Peter Mitchell)

Most of the existing 1950's rebuilds of post-war vehicles were withdrawn following the route no. 60 conversion. This included no. 562, seen climbing Spaines Road from Fartown Bar on a Sunday morning route 10 journey from Brackenhall via Birkby on 2 February 1964. It is crossing the Wasp Nest Road junction–these workings did not use the Birkby turning loop.
(Vic Nutton/Travel Lens Photographic)

Also withdrawn at this time were nos. 568 and 572, seen side by side in St George's Square. (Vic Nutton/Travel lens Photographic)

Another Town Centre Routeing Change...

From 26 March 1964, a few weeks after the Crosland Hill route conversion, there was another major change to the town centre wiring. On Outcote Bank, Manchester Street and Market Street the wiring was removed owing to the impending closure and subsequent obliteration of Manchester Street as part of the new Civic Centre development. Trolleybuses on the last remaining Manchester Road route from Longwood therefore reverted to using the wiring between Outcote Bank and Chapel Hill, not used for regular public service since 1947. To allow unimpeded progress for Bradley trolleys in John William Street, a wiring loop was erected at the Brackenhall and Riddings queue stands.

...and Another Nail in the Coffin

At the end of January 1965, the timetabled Moldgreen to Marsh route no. 72 workings were withdrawn, being replaced by yet another Corporation motorbus service. However, some workings to both turning points did continue to run at peak hours.

In the mid-1950s, Outcote Bank was widened for two-way traffic. No. 570 is seen turning off Manchester Road during these works, which entailed building a new retaining wall on the right. Note the view over Longroyd Bridge in the background. (Roy Brook/Paul Watson)

In Market Street no. 604 is passing the ABC Cinema. Built in 1936 as the Ritz, it was renamed in 1961. Its finest hour was probably when it played host to a live Beatles concert in November 1963. Closure came in 1983 and the site is now a supermarket. In this view, it is showing 'The VIPs', a 1963 drama starring Richard Burton and Elizabeth Taylor. (Vic Nutton/Travel Lens Photographic)

By 1964, no. 596 was the last of its type to retain the dipped mudguards over the rear wheels and it was to lose this feature when overhauled later in the year. It is about to cross the Market Place junction from Westgate into Kirkgate in June 1964. (Author)

This seasonal scene of the Market Place shows no. 599 in New Street passing the Christmas tree. 19 December 1964. (Bas Longbottom)

'The End of an Era'

Although the trolleybus conversion scheme was considerably shortened (by about five years), the Corporation seemed in no rush to replace its trolleybuses. The conversion of the town routes from 1964 generally took place at the rate of one through service per year, an annual order being placed for the replacement motorbuses. The final four conversions took place on the same week each year. During this period there was never any attempt to partially convert any route (e.g. on weekends) and it was practically unheard of under normal circumstances for a motorbus to be seen operating on a designated trolleybus service.

The fall of the trolleybuses – route by route *(showing the number of vehicles remaining in service **after** each conversion)*		
8th November 1961	Town Centre to West Vale	120
30th January 1963	Town Centre to Marsden	92
5th February 1964	Birkby to Crosland Hill	76
14th July 1965	Almondbury to Fixby	52
13th July 1966	Lockwood to Brackenhall	---
13th July 1966	Newsome to Riddings	35
12th July 1967	Bradley to Longwood	20
13th July 1968	Waterloo to Lindley and Outlane	Nil

The Moldgreen loop was a third of a mile long and most of these journeys ran through the town to Marsh or Salendine Nook. This late 1950s view shows no. 618 which has just turned off Wakefield Road into Broad Lane. (Roy Brook/Paul Watson)

The Marsh loop turned off the Lindley route at Acre Street into Wellington Street and Gibson Street, where it joined the Outlane route wiring just west of the Bay Horse junction of the Lindley/Outlane routes. No. 494 is seen in Gibson Street in the late 1950s. (Peter Mitchell)

In their last months of existence, Almondbury route trolleybuses had to negotiate the extensive roadworks at the junction of Somerset Road and Wakefield Road. This view shows the scene in August 1964, just before work started. No. 554 is in Somerset Road with the Wakefield Road junction and the Lyceum cinema, shortly to be demolished, in the background. (Bas Longbottom)

No. 618 is running through what appears to be a rough track on a building site. Wakefield Road is in the background and the demolished Lyceum Cinema site is on the right. (Roy Brook/Paul Watson)

Several vehicle types were withdrawn after the Almondbury/Fixby conversion. This included the last pair of trolleys with original Park Royal bodies. In this busy scene at Smithy, no. 590 is approaching the junction from the Fixby direction. Note the Hillman Imp on the left.
25 March 1965.
(Bas Longbottom)

Also taken out of service at this time were the last of the 1950s rebuilds on post-war chassis. Roe bodied no. 580 is seen in Northgate on driver training duties in May 1965, just two months before withdrawal. It is about to turn right into Northumberland Street. Unusually, this view was taken on a Saturday afternoon – such training was normally a weekday activity. Note the board fixed to the platform step which warned that the vehicle was not in public service and should not be boarded. (Author)

No. 593, the first of the 1950 Sunbeams, was withdrawn from service after operating the last ever trolleybus journey from Almondbury. Here it is seen in Bradford Road having just left the Fartown Bar stop on its way into town, showing an incorrect destination. It was overhauled as late as September 1964, losing its front bumper in the process.
(Peter Mitchell)

Most of the 1950 Sunbeams ran until route nos. 10 and 20 were converted in 1966. No. 604 is seen in Bradley Boulevard, Brackenhall. (Roy Brook/Paul Watson)

On the Riddings route, no. 631 has reached the top of Woodhouse Hill and is about to turn into Chestnut Street towards the Riddings estate. (Peter Mitchell)

The Beaumont Street Flyer

The Gas Works railway, locally known as the 'Beaumont Street Flyer', was another Huddersfield institution that disappeared in the1960s. It opened in 1922, and connected the Corporation gas works at Leeds Road with the Newtown railway sidings alongside St John's Road. Most of the line was along the street, running the full length of Beaumont Street, with open level crossings controlled by a flagman, over Leeds Road and Bradford Road. A pair of Barclays-built saddle tank steam locomotives handled the trains of coal wagons for most of the line's existence, although diesel locomotives were used in the 1960s, by which time it was run by the North Eastern Gas Board. Closure of the line came in 1966. (See also page 135)

North Eastern Gas Board locomotive no. 2, having brought its train along Beaumont Street from Leeds Road, is crossing the Bradford Road/Northgate junction beneath the trolleybus wires. From here it will pass under the railway viaduct and climb up to the Newtown sidings. 28 September 1962. (P. Eckersley/Author's collection)

An anticlockwise wiring loop serving the Great Northern Street works turned off Northgate into Beaumont Street, ran in front of the works, then returned to Bradford Road via Ray Street. The loop was popular on enthusiasts' tours of the system, and on one such an occasion, no. 541 is seen parked adjacent to the Beaumont Street railway track, which can be seen crossing Bradford Road before passing under the railway viaduct. May 1962. (Jim Copland/Paul Watson)

The long climb up Newsome Road is evident in this classic 1950s view of no. 558 at the Tunnacliffe Road stop. A panorama of Huddersfield, town centre and beyond, is in the background. (Roy Brook/Paul Watson)

The industrial area around Folly Hall, near the bottom of Chapel Hill forms the backdrop to this view of no. 496 on Lockwood Road. (Peter Mitchell)

At the foot of Newsome Road was the River Colne bridge at King's Mill. A 1950 Sunbeam is reflected in the water as it crosses on its way to town. (Bas Longbottom)

No. 610 passes the shops in Keldregate, just before it makes the turn into Brooklands. (Peter Mitchell)

This is another classic 1950s view on the trolleybus system. No 613 is in Longwood village, showing the stone-sett paved roadway and the War Memorial. (Roy Brook/Paul Watson)

The conversion of the Longwood-Bradley route marked the end in service of the 1960s rebuilds with new East Lancashire bodies, some of these being only five years old. The very last in service was Karrier no. 548, which ran until a couple of days before the conversion date. By then it was the last Huddersfield trolleybus to carry the Karrier name. In this earlier view, it is seen in Longwood village approaching the terminus. (Peter Mitchell)

In the latter half of 1967, all the redundant town centre wiring north of Northumberland Street was removed. Wiring along Byram Street from Kirkgate was retained, and a new curve was erected turning left from Byram Street into Northumberland Street, opposite the Transport Offices. No 628 is seen using this curve during an enthusiasts' tour on the last Sunday of trolleybus operation. 7 July 1968. (Author)

This typical scene in Southgate during the final year of the trolleybus system, depicts both types of vehicle which operated to the end. Sunbeam no. 633 leads BUT no. 626 into the town centre. Shore Head roundabout is in the left background, and beyond that, under construction, is the Huddersfield Polytechnic sports hall. (Author's collection)

Another view from the final year of operation shows trolleybuses passing at the highest point on the system, Leeches Hill, Outlane. Sunbeam no. 632, is just departing from the stop as BUT no. 630, which is about to descend the hill into Outlane, passes in the opposite direction. (Roy Brook/Paul Watson)

Decorated no. 623 is ablaze with light as it stands at the Waterloo stop in Westgate. (Roy Brook)

The Last Rites

The Corporation made considerable provision to commemorate the end of the town's trolleybuses. In the final week, all trolleybus conductors issued special, printed 'Last Trolleybus Week' tickets from their normal 'Ultimate' machines, and a small illustrated brochure describing the 68 years of electric traction in the town was issued. Most impressive of all was the provision of a decorated and illuminated trolleybus, BUT no 623, which entered public service in this form on the last Monday of operation. Creating much favourable attention from the public, especially during the hours of darkness, it would be the official 'last trolleybus' carrying the Civic party on the following Saturday.

During the final week, trolleybuses went about their normal business, and Friday 12 July was the last day of full normal service. The following day, motorbuses took over the last routes, with only a token trolleybus presence, which ceased during the afternoon.

The last normal service journey on Friday, the 11.30pm Town to Salendine Nook and return, was operated by Sunbeam no. 638 and driven by Robert Collinson, who was to drive the last public trolleybus on the following day. Hugh Taylor recorded the event in an article for 'Trolleybus Magazine'.

'Colly' was driving, and at the reverser he put up on his destination blind '92 Thornton Lodge'. He always did this (on depot journeys), so that you knew he was coming! From Salendine Nook to depot I had an unforgettable journey. Vivid flashes were made, with power drawn from frogs and crossings. Breakers were tripped

twice, someone swiped the bamboo pole, and on the driver's own initiative, 638 returned to depot via Byram Street instead of Railway Street. Enthusiasts were cheering the driver – singing 'Auld Lang Syne' and 'For he's a jolly good fellow'.

On the last day that trolleybuses ran, Saturday 13 July, events were more formal. Only two trolleybuses were turned out for service, no. 640 on route 71 and no. 629 on route 73. The latter would be the last public trolleybus when it left Westgate at 2.31pm for the final round trip to Waterloo and Outlane. During the morning, an old friend returned, this being the preserved no. 541, which operated a tour for National Trolleybus Association members. At midday no. 640 broke down in Westgate and was replaced for the last two trips to Lindley by no. 638, which had been parked in St George's Square in time-honoured fashion. By this time no. 629 was running with a full standing load of passengers, all intent on being on board to the bitter end. It became evident that the demand for a last ride required more trolleybuses to be put into service, and consequently from 1.30pm, each trip saw a further relief vehicle added. When no. 629 departed Westgate for Outlane at 3pm, it was preceded by three vehicles. Following behind all of these was no. 623 carrying the Civic party, and driven by C.P. Jones, who was also retiring that day. This was seen off at 2.31pm by crowds lining Westgate, comprising both locals and well wishers from all over the country. Crowds were out again when Outlane was reached, and the vehicles set off for the last time into Huddersfield. On reaching St George's Square, no one alighted from no. 629, and it was allowed to

Operating a tour on the very last day of trolleybus operation, no. 541 passes the preserved Huddersfield wartime austerity Daimler motorbus at Oakes. At the time, these were the only preserved Huddersfield Corporation vehicles. (Author's collection)

In St George's Square, no. 638 waits after operating the last trolleybus journey to Lindley until called upon at 3pm to duplicate the last trolleybus journey to Outlane. On the left decorated no. 623 loads its civic guests before departing to Waterloo just after 2.30pm. A trolleybus replacement Daimler Fleetline motorbus passes by on the right, operating on the Birkby route. (John Meredith)

On the last day, the final round trip for no. 629 was scheduled to leave Westgate for Waterloo at 2.31pm. Prior to this more trolleys were brought into service to run in front, and no. 629 would then be followed by illuminated no. 623 carrying civic guests. Here, at 2.24pm, no. 626 loads in Westgate, and this view gives an indication of the crowds that were gathering. In the background is no. 627, another trolley brought out to cope with demand, and behind that is no. 629. 13 July 1968. (Peter Thompson)

73

return to Longroyd Bridge with its passengers, passing the Saturday afternoon shoppers in New Street. Another crowd was waiting outside the doorway of the depot, where the passengers very reluctantly took their leave before it silently moved into the building. By this time no. 623 was disgorging its party in the town centre (Buxton Road), prior to being towed away to Great Northern Street Works where an open day was being held.

Mike Russell, the editor of 'Trolleybus Magazine' introduced the article describing the closure thus:

"A trolleybus closure more moving than that which took place high up on the Pennines on 13 July 1968 is hard to imagine. An air of extreme nostalgia prevailed in the village of Outlane on this dismal Saturday, when Huddersfield's very last trolleybuses ran on their final journeys into the town centre and brought to an end nearly 35 years of operation on one of the finest trolleybus networks that these islands have ever known. For Huddersfield's closure was enshrouded in sentiment of a kind which has never revealed itself at a trolleybus conversion."

The end is nigh for no. 629, as it passes Wellington Mill, Oakes, making its last journey into town from Outlane, packed with mourning trolleybus fans. (Jim Copland/Paul Watson)

After performing its 'Last Trolleybus' duties, no. 623 turns from St George's Square into John William Street shortly before the civic party alight to take refreshments at the Town Hall. (R.S. Ledgard)

HUDDERSFIELD TROLLEYBUSES IN COLOUR

Trolleys in the Early 1950s

Pre-war Karrier no. 527 is seen in John William Street on 23 September 1950. (Clarence Carter/Online Transport Archive)

The first post-war trolley, no. 541, is at St George's Square on 23 September 1950. (Clarence Carter/Online Transport Archive)

This vehicle, the first of the 1950 delivery of Sunbeams was displayed at the Commercial Motor Show in 1950. It was given special embellishments including red bumpers and gold lining for the occasion. (Charles H. Roe Ltd / colour added by Malcolm Fraser)

Seen at Bradley Bar in the summer of 1955 is Karrier MS2 no. 561. It is standing at the stop on the main Huddersfield to Bradford Road having just joined the latter from Fixby Road. (Jim Copland/Malcolm King)

Town Centre

St George's Square

St George's Square, surrounded by some of Huddersfield's most eminent buildings, was one of the main town centre focal points of the trolley system.

It was common practice for a spare trolley to be parked in the Square, even on Christmas Day. In this scene, one of the eight MS2 type trolleys rebuilt in the early 1960s is seen standing with its poles down. In accordance with regulations, a wooden chock has been placed against the off-side front wheel of the vehicle. In the background is the architecturally-acclaimed railway station, and for travellers coming to the town by train, this was likely to be their first sight of a Huddersfield trolleybus. The traction poles in this area were painted a very light green shade, rather than the normal dark green. Note the bubble car in front of the GPO van in the background. 8 June 1966. (Marcus Eavis/Online Transport Archive)

This view looks in the opposite direction and shows trolley no. 601 standing amongst the daffodils. The large building behind it is the George Hotel, whose stonework had recently been cleaned. In the background a trolley can be seen in John William Street. It is about to pass the head office of the Corporation Transport Department at the top of Northumberland Street. 30 April 1966. (David Clarke)

No. 576 is negotiating the east side of the Square, and will travel along Railway Street to Westgate, in order to take up service to Outlane. It is probably working a tea-time extra journey. The Lion Buildings in John William Street are prominent in the background, surmounted by the Lion itself. On the right are Britannia Buildings, then home to the Huddersfield Building Society. No. 576 was one of this type which had its front bumper removed, leaving a very short front dash panel which resulted in a 'mini-skirt' look. 5 September 1962. (Tony Belton)

The railway station and George Hotel are again prominent in this view of trolley no. 544 turning left from the Square into John William Street bound for Birkby. This un-rebuilt vehicle, together with no. 541, retained its three aperture front destination layout. The remaining five un-rebuilt vehicles of this type were given centralised indicators when overhauled in early 1961. 5 September 1962. (Tony Belton)

Viaduct Street

Trolleys on the Bradford Road routes (Brackenhall, Riddings and Fixby), entered the town centre via Viaduct Street. The railway viaduct carries the main Trans-Pennine railway line into West Yorkshire.

Trolley no. 549 (un-rebuilt and with centralised destination indicators) is seen at the junction of Viaduct Street and John William Street, looking along the former street to the junction with Bradford Road. There appears to be white smoke from a steam locomotive on the viaduct. On the right is the car showroom of Rippon Bros, suppliers of Rolls Royce and Bentley cars to the wealthy mill owners in the town. (Fred Ivey)

A different angle of the scene at the junction of Viaduct Street and John William Street shows, on the left, the railway bridge over St John's Road, underneath which ran the Birkby route trolleys. The raised footway under the bridge is a consequence of the roadway being lowered in the mid-1930s to allow trolleybus operation. No. 632, one of the newest Huddersfield trolleybuses dating from 1959, turns into John William Street on a journey from Fixby. Note the prominent advertisement on the bridge for Rippon Bros, complete with pointing 'hand'. 7 September 1962. (Tony Belton)

On a journey from Birkby, no. 549 emerges from the bridge into John William Street. In 1963 this vehicle acquired a new bright metal windscreen surround. 25 January 1964. (Alan Dixon/Paul Watson)

John William Street

All the main town centre stops for trolleys heading south along John William Street were located along the section between Northumberland Street and New Street. In order, from north to south these were Newsome, Crosland Hill, Marsden, Lockwood and Longwood.
Despite this, there were no loops in the overhead wiring to allow trolleys to overtake each other.

Trolleys coming from Bradford Road and Birkby set down passengers at an alighting-only stop just south of Brook Street. No. 541 is seen here in front of the Rice Bowl, the town's first Chinese restaurant. No. 568 is loading at the Bradley stop at the side of the George Hotel. From here, Bradley-bound trolleys turned right into Brook Street on the corner of which the Empire Cinema can be seen.
5 September 1962.
(Tony Belton)

This scene at the Bradley stop looks south, and shows no. 590 loading for the ICI works in the morning peak hour (8.20am by the Transport Office clock). Note that there were separate wires here for the Bradley trolleys and these crossed over the Bradford Road / Birkby wires into Brook Street. The Corporation motor bus on the left is operating on the Birkby to Balmoral Avenue route. It was originally planned that trolleybuses would operate along Balmoral Avenue as an extension to the Crosland Hill route. (Fred Ivey)

Passing the top of Northumberland Street, with the Corporation Transport office in the background, is trolley no. 543. The Yorkshire Evening News Austin van bears a registration number that today would be extremely desirable. (Nick Hirst)

Trolleys from Bradley entered the town centre via Northumberland Street. In this view, no. 542 sweeps round the corner into John William Street, the junction being under the control of a policeman on point duty. In the left background is the Princess Cinema, closed in 1984, and in the far distance can be seen the Ibbotson Flats under construction. A Corporation Transport Austin van is parked beside the Transport Offices. 28 August 1963. (Tony Belton)

Another scene at the top of Northumberland Street shows no. 607 working on a tea-time special duty. It has probably come from the ICI works on Leeds Road, and, having dropped its passengers, is now getting in position for its next journey to Birkby Hall Road, a short working of the Birkby route, where it will pick up workers from the Hopkinson's valve works. The limitations of the overhead wiring layout in the town centre will require this vehicle to turn in St George's Square, thereby missing out the main Birkby stop in Railway Street. 28 August 1963. (Tony Belton)

Until 1964, only the Brackenhall and Riddings services ran along John William Street in a northerly direction between Westgate and St George's Square. No. 582, one of the last batch of trolleys to be rebuilt with a new body, is seen coasting over the frogs and crossings leading into St George's Square, having just started a journey to Riddings. 21 February 1963. (Tony Belton)

Turning into St George's Square from John William Street, this trolley is on its way to Westgate from Bradley, to work a morning school special journey to Salendine Nook. Many of these journeys worked through from outer termini. Note the group of Huddersfield New College pupils making their way to the Salendine Nook stop in Westgate. 7 July 1967. (David Pearson)

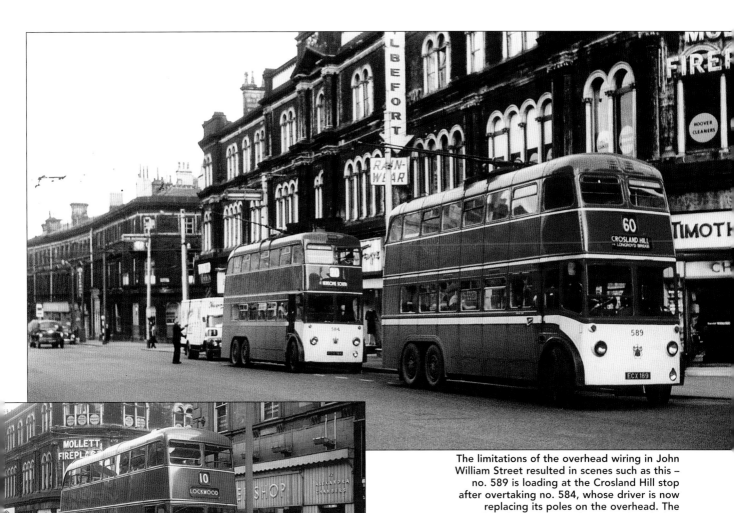

The limitations of the overhead wiring in John William Street resulted in scenes such as this – no. 589 is loading at the Crosland Hill stop after overtaking no. 584, whose driver is now replacing its poles on the overhead. The Timothy Whites chemist shop was closed after the takeover of the company by Boots in 1968. 5 February 1964. (Alan Dixon/Paul Watson)

Here, no. 625 is waiting as the driver of the trolley in front (at the Marsden stop) pulls down the poles to allow it to move up to the Lockwood stop. (H. Luff)

No. 567, caked in winter road dirt, waits to depart from the Marsden stop before its seven mile journey along the Colne Valley on the last day of trolleybus operation on the route. 30 January 1963. (Alan Dixon/Paul Watson).

After the route re-organisation of 1963, the Longwood route was renumbered from 90 to 40. No. 601 is at the Longwood stop on route 40. These vehicles were the last type to have conventional cab doors, all bodies built after 1951 having sliding doors. The driver has omitted to change the destination blind, which is incorrectly showing 'Bradley via Deighton'. This blind predates the opening of the Bradley Keldregate route extension, new ones after this event having 'Bradley via Keldregate' or 'Bradley via Leeds Road' displays to differentiate the two Bradley termini.
(A. Swain/David Hall)

The stops for the Bradford Road routes to Brackenhall and Riddings were situated together on the west side of John William Street. No. 550 is seen pulling away from the Riddings stop, whilst an Armstrong – Siddeley car tries to overtake in defiance of the trolley driver's hand signal. 5th September 1962.
(Tony Belton)

In this view, no. 609 on the Bradley service has passed the Bradford Road stops as it approaches the Bradley stop at the other side of St George's Square. The end of the loop erected in 1964 is evident in the right background.
(Author's collection)

In March 1964, trolleys from Longwood towards Bradley were rerouted in the town centre to run via New Street and John William Street. A wiring loop was therefore erected for the Brackenhall and Riddings stops, operated by a pull frog, allowing Bradley trolleys to overtake on their way to the Bradley stop at the side of the George Hotel. This very common scene at the time, although rarely photographed, shows the turbanned conductor of no. 631 'pulling the trigger' at this point on the last day of the 10 and 20 trolleybus services. Seen opposite, at the Lockwood stop, is no. 603, which would be withdrawn from the fleet later that day after the evening peak service. 13 July 1966. (Author)

Trolley no. 636, en route for Cowlersley, is about to go through the traffic lights and cross into New Street in this busy scene. (Peter Grace / John Laker)

New Street

New Street, now a pedestrian area, is one of the main shopping streets in the town.

At the southern end of John William Street is the intersection where Westgate crosses over into Kirkgate at the Market Place. New Street, extending south towards Chapel Hill, starts at this point. Trolleys returning to Longroyd Bridge Depot from the Kirkgate direction used a wiring connection turning left into New Street. Here, no. 628 performs this manoeuvre during the last week of trolleybus operation. By this time the wires in John William Street and New Street were only used by trolleys to or from the depot. The running man on the right is Philip Jenkinson, a contributor to this book. 12 July 1968. (Mike Russell)

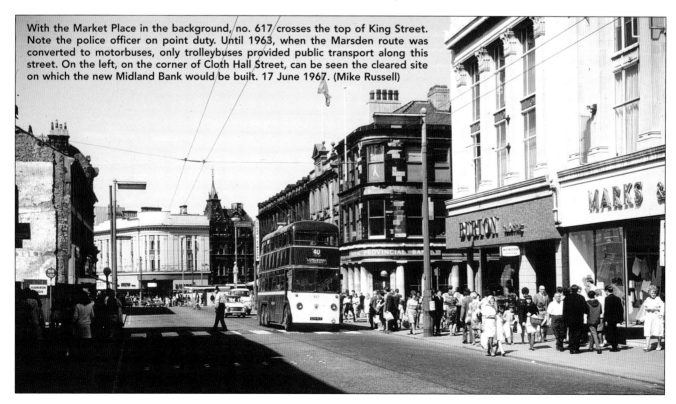

With the Market Place in the background, no. 617 crosses the top of King Street. Note the police officer on point duty. Until 1963, when the Marsden route was converted to motorbuses, only trolleybuses provided public transport along this street. On the left, on the corner of Cloth Hall Street, can be seen the cleared site on which the new Midland Bank would be built. 17 June 1967. (Mike Russell)

On a Sunday afternoon in 1955, no. 565, still with its original Park Royal body, pauses at the Lockwood stop outside Woolworths. (Jim Copland / Malcolm King collection)

Just a few yards further along, at the junction with Ramsden Street, no. 619 passes Woods music shop. It is crossing into what was then called Buxton Road, later absorbed into New Street. 17 June 1967. (Mike Russell)

Having just turned on to Manchester Road from Buxton Road, no. 618 pauses at the stop here. At the time of this photograph (1955), it was the highest numbered member of the fleet. In the background is the Co-operative store. (Jim Copland/Malcolm King)

A similar scene to the previous photograph, but after the roundabout was installed at the top of Chapel Hill. No. 615 completes the negotiation of the Chapel Hill roundabout as it turns on to Manchester Road. 19 May 1964. (Roland Box)

Market Street /Westgate

This scene shows no. 529 about to cross Westgate from Market Street into Railway Street, having come from the depot via Outcote Bank and Market Street. Behind is no. 632 on the Birkby service. The wiring connection on the right turning into Westgate was erected in May 1960, allowing trolleys to gain access to the Marsh direction without the complicated round-town movement previously necessary. This was particularly useful for the many journeys provided for schoolchildren to and from Salendine Nook Schools. (Stanley King – colour added by Malcolm Fraser)

Railway Street

In Railway Street there was a long metal and brick shelter dating from the early 1950s used by the Birkby and Fixby services. Each service was provided with a loop, allowing trolleys on the Bradley route to pass, as well as workings from the depot. At the southern end was the Birkby stop, where no. 523 is seen in the 1950s. (Phil Tatt/Online Transport Archive)

Brook Street

Bradley trolleys left the town centre via Brook Street where the wholesale fruit and vegetable market was situated. The street could become quite congested, and no. 615 is seen picking its way through the parked vehicles. It is about to negotiate the trailing frog of the wires from Byram Street, used by football specials to the Leeds Road ground (see photo on page 46 (top). 17 June 1967. (Mike Russell)

No. 615 is at the bottom of Brook Street, turning into Northgate. Originally the route crossed Northgate here and continued straight on into Union Street to reach Leeds Road. From late 1960 the route was diverted into Northgate to reach Leeds Road at the new roundabout at the junction with Northumberland Street. Note the remains of the former wiring connection turning left into Northgate – this was used by football specials to the Fartown ground, and to access the Great Northern Street Works. 17 June 1967. (Mike Russell)

Northgate

No. 609, on a tea-time extra working to pick up workers from the ICI Works, has just turned from Brook Street onto the recently widened part of Northgate. In the distance, along Northgate, is the bridge under the viaduct leading to Bradford Road. The Northgate wires were used by the recently introduced Fixby to Almondbury service, and no. 609 will effectively cross these to take the left-hand turn into Leeds Road at Northumberland Street roundabout. 28 August 1963. (Tony Belton)

Northumberland Street

No. 546 is coming round the new Northumberland Street roundabout, opened in late 1960, and is heading for the town centre in the approximate position of the photograph of no. 583 on page 51 (top). Behind are the Richmond Flats, one of a trio of high-rise dwellings built at this location in 1962. The trolley is about to pass under the trailing frog of the wires from Northgate, used by the inbound Fixby service. 22 April 1965. (Mike Russell)

Climbing Northumberland Street is no. 590, with the Ibbotson Flats in the background. On the left is the facing frog and turnout allowing route 34 trolleys from Fixby to turn into Lord Street. (Author's collection)

Until early 1963, when it was moved to Lord Street, the town centre stop for the Almondbury service was in Byram Street, near the junction with St Peter's Street. Here no. 627 is seen on a route 33 working and on departure will turn right into St Peter's Street to run down to Southgate, which was a continuation of Northgate. 5 September 1962. (Tony Belton)

The Byram Street stop previously used by Almondbury trolleys was, from the end of January 1963, used by trolleys working on new route 34 from Almondbury to Fixby. No. 630 is seen at the stop shortly after the change was introduced. 21 February 1963. (Tony Belton)

A feature of the Fixby route from 1960 was the operation of school special journeys to Bradley Bar. In this view, no. 632 is in Byram Street prior to picking up schoolchildren at the Fixby stop, and the driver is lowering its poles to allow no. 612 to pass on its way to the Almondbury stop in Lord Street. (Fred Ivey)

Northgate to Lord Street

The new arrangements for the Fixby service involved using the wiring on Northgate between Bradford Road and Northumberland Street, previously used to allow access for trolleybuses to Great Northern Street Works. In this view no. 600 is approaching the junction with Brook Street, where it will cross the Bradley route wiring, then turn right at the Northumberland Street roundabout into the town centre. There was an automatic frog here to enable this manoeuvre.
28 August 1963. (Tony Belton)

The use of trolleybuses along Lord Street lasted only 2½ years, and this view of no. 581 at the Almondbury stop in Lord Street was taken on the last day of operation. Note the setted road surface and motorbuses from the County, Yorkshire Traction and Corporation (JOC) fleets.
14 July 1965. (Author)

Northgate to Southgate and Rosemary Lane

Wiring was provided to allow trolleybuses to run southwards from Northumberland Street towards Southgate. This was joined at the bottom of St Peter's Street with the wires of the Almondbury trolleys. At the junction of Kirkgate and Southgate there was a short length of road leading from the north end of Southgate into Kirkgate known as Rosemary Lane. Until 1962, there was a wiring curve here turning right from Southgate into Westgate which enabled trolleys entering service on the Lindley, Outlane and West Vale routes to access Kirkgate and Westgate. When additional wiring curves were erected in the Railway Street/Westgate area by 1962, this link was dismantled.

This trolleybus, no. 634, is working on a tea-time-special duty, and is positioning itself to run a journey to Salendine Nook Schools from Westgate. Having negotiated the Northumberland Street roundabout, it is proceeding along Northgate towards Southgate, where it will turn into Kirkgate at Rosemary Lane. In the left background another trolleybus can be seen emerging from Brook Street. 27 March 1962. (Alan Dixon/Paul Watson)

Parked at Rosemary Lane is no. 613, its crew enjoying a break before taking up service. In the background, behind the Southgate Hotel, is the new Telephone Exchange building. 13 May 1961. (Alan Dixon/Paul Watson)

Southgate

Trolleys on the Wakefield Road routes (Waterloo, Moldgreen and Almondbury) used Southgate to access Wakefield Road. In the early 1960s this road widened as part of the Inner Ring Road scheme and a new roundabout was constructed at Shore Head (the town end of Wakefield Road).

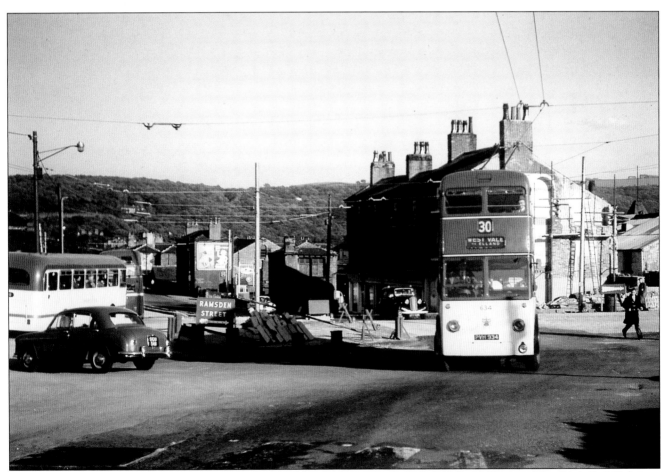

This is the scene at the site of the new Shore Head roundabout, looking towards Wakefield Road. The roundabout is in its initial stage of construction and no. 634 coming from Almondbury is negotiating its way through the site. A Yorkshire Traction single deck bus is on the left. 19 June 1961. (Alan Dixon/Paul Watson)

This view looking in the opposite direction from the previous photo shows no. 635, which has strayed too far from the new line of overhead wiring and has consequently dewired. The crew are at the rear trying to retrieve the errant trolley poles whilst a policeman is dealing with a motorist who is apparently confused by the new traffic system (which is possibly why the trolley was forced away from the wires). 8 July 1961. (Alan Dixon/Paul Watson)

The completed Southgate roundabout is shown here. No. 631 on the left has paused to allow no. 638 onto the roundabout from Oldgate. Trolleys leaving the town centre were diverted onto the latter street from 1963. This view was taken during the last week of trolley operation and on the last day in service for no. 631. 11 July 1968. (Mike Russell)

Looking north along Southgate, the widening of this road is underway in this scene. This carriageway would become entirely northbound, and the new southbound carriageway is on the right. Note that bracket arms have been erected here in anticipation of outbound trolleys being diverted onto the new road. This never happened because no provision was made to access the southbound carriageway from Kirkgate. Instead outbound trolleys were diverted on to Oldgate from 21 July 1963, and no. 632 is seen here on the last day that the southbound wires here were used. 20 July 1963. (Alan Dixon/Paul Watson)

Oldgate

From July 1963 outbound trolleys were diverted from Southgate onto Oldgate, which runs parallel with Southgate as far as the new Shore Head roundabout. A new stop was provided at the Kirkgate end of Oldgate, and here no. 541, having just turned off Kirkgate, is about to pick up passengers. Its badly set via blind shows (partly) 'via Edgerton', used for the former West Vale route. 28 August 1963. (Tony Belton)

This scene in Oldgate shows two trolleys, with no. 579 leading. They will shortly turn left to reach Shore Head roundabout. (Hugh Taylor)

Kirkgate

Trolleys from Almondbury turned right from Kirkgate into Byram Street immediately after passing the entrance to the Parish Church. The facing frog for this manoeuvre was placed well in advance of the turn (near Lord Street) and there was a lengthy stretch of double wiring. No. 555 turns into Byram Street, whilst no. 590 passes on the nearside. (Fred Ivey)

At the western end of Kirkgate was the crossing with John William Street and New Street. Here no. 588 crosses into Westgate. This vehicle subsequently received centralised destination indicators when overhauled in 1961. (Roy Brook/Leeds Transport Historical Society)

Crossing from Westgate into Kirkgate is no. 633. On the right is Rushworth's department store, with its distinctive revolving clock above the doorway. 7 July 1968. (Mike Russell)

Westgate

The West Vale stop was in Westgate, just west of the New Street junction. A wiring loop was provided for vehicles standing here. This view shows no. 578 loading at the stop outside the Wellington Hotel. 4 November 1961. (Alan Dixon/Paul Watson)

No. 493 was the last trolley to run over any part of the West Vale route. It is seen prior to departing on the 11.30pm journey to Birchencliffe. 8 November 1961. (Alan Dixon/Paul Watson)

No. 543, in its last month of service before withdrawal, stands at the Waterloo stop near the junction with Railway Street. The shop behind the shelter was John Manners gentlemen's outfitters and suppliers of school uniforms. 2 June 1967. (David Pearson)

In 1962 curves were erected to allow trolleys to turn right from Railway Street leading directly to the Lindley/Outlane stops at the west end of Westgate, and a corresponding curve left from Kirkgate into Railway Street. This greatly assisted in the flexibility of operations, particularly the many school specials operating to and from Salendine Nook. Seen turning from Railway Street into Westgate is no. 578. In the background a BUT trolley is turning left to reach the Waterloo stop. (Tony Belton)

Seen turning from Westgate into Railway Street is no. 594, having just completed a school special journey from Salendine Nook. Before this curve was erected, it was common, if unofficial, practice for trolleys to coast around this corner. (Vic Nutton – colour added by Malcolm Fraser)

The West Vale route branched off at Westgate to run up New North Road. Looking east down Westgate, no. 560 is seen entering New North Road, with the main Lindley and Outlane stops visible to the right. Note the string of 'fairy lights' just to the left of the vehicle – these were provided at wide junctions and switched on during periods of poor visibility eg fog. 28 October 1961. (Alan Dixon/Paul Watson)

No. 628 is seen at the Outlane stop in Westgate outside the
Wah Yan Chinese restaurant before setting off on an evening
journey to Salendine Nook. 27 October 1967. (David Pearson)

Departing from the Westgate stop on a journey to Outlane is no. 596. It
is actually passing over the railway tunnel at the southern end of
Huddersfield station. In the background is Whiteleys Café. (Nick Hirst)

Brighouse

Converted from trams	30 June 1940
Route length	6 miles
Service linked to	Lockwood (1942-7), then Longwood
Closed to trolleybuses (Brighouse to Fixby)	8 July 1955
Last vehicle over route	563

This rare colour image shows no. 570 climbing Ogden Lane at Rastrick. In the background at the foot of the hill is the Rastrick short working reversing triangle. (Malcolm King collection)

West Vale

Converted from trams	28 May 1939
Route length	5 miles
Service linked to	Almondbury
Closed to trolleybuses	8 November 1961
Last vehicle over whole route	640
(subsequently 493 to Birchencliffe)	

No. 574 is at the terminal stop in Stainland Road. Until 1934, Halifax Corporation trams ran along here on the route to Stainland. 29 June 1961. (Alan Dixon/Paul Watson)

No. 547 stands at the terminus. It received a modernised destination indicator layout when overhauled in 1961.
(H. Luff/Online Transport Archive)

The houses of West Vale form the background to this view of no. 614 climbing out of the village and onto Long Wall, which ran along the valley side, 29 June 1961. (Alan Dixon/Paul Watson)

Climbing Victoria Road in Elland is no. 574. The narrow roadway here requires the use of bracket arm suspension. Note the 'Trolleybus Fare Stage' sign on the traction pole. Stage 20 was for Burley Street or Town Hall, a 6d ride into Huddersfield. 8 November 1961. (Alan Dixon/Paul Watson)

There was a short working turning loop at Elland (route no. 31), which was used by peak-hour extra journeys from Huddersfield. No. 637 has turned off Victoria Road into Elizabeth Street at the Market Place. Note that there was also wiring provision to turn into here from the West Vale direction (to the right), but this link, once deployed on Elland market days, was latterly very rarely used, and the corresponding wiring link leading back towards West Vale at the Town Hall was removed when the roundabout was constructed there in the late 1950s. 12 May 1961. (Alan Dixon/Paul Watson)

One of the last trolleys to use the Elland short working loop was no. 611, seen here in Elizabeth Street on the last evening of operation. 8 November 1961. (Alan Dixon/Paul Watson)

The Elland turning loop wires turned right from Elizabeth Street into Huddersfield Road. No. 573 is seen here, and the wires turning out of Elizabeth Street are just visible in the background. The Town Hall is on the left and the vehicle is about to rejoin the main route here.
5 July 1961. (Alan Dixon /Paul Watson)

At Elland Town Hall, seen on the left, trolleys from West Vale turned onto Huddersfield Road at the roundabout. No. 548 is passing under the trailing frog of the short-working loop. 4 November 1961. (David Clarke)

The route towards Huddersfield from Elland involved the ascent to the top of The Ainleys, a steep climb including a sharp bend. On the descent into Elland, the coasting brake was required to be used. Seen approaching Elland is no. 636, under the bridge at Sharratt's brickworks. This point was at the end of the coasting-brake section, and the vehicle has come to a stand at the stop here for the brake to be disengaged. 28 June 1961. Alan Dixon/Paul Watson)

Here no. 569 is seen ascending towards Ainley Top. Trolleys could climb the hill faster than any other vehicle, especially motorbuses on the trunk route from Halifax. 28 June 1961. (Alan Dixon/Paul Watson)

The coasting-brake resulted in a sedate descent at no more than 15mph. No. 556 is seen here, being passed by other traffic. (E.C. Bennett/Online Transport Archive)

107

Just beyond the cutting leading from the bridges at Ainley Top towards Huddersfield, there was a short working turning circle at Branch Lane. Here, no. 570 is being repaired following a dewirement which has bent the trolley poles. Derrick no. A9, an AEC Mandator, is drawn up behind to allow the overhead linesmen to access the roof of the vehicle. One of them is straightening the nearside (negative) pole, whilst the other is attending to the trolley head. The Birchencliffe turning loop (route no. 32) can be seen in the background, this having replaced the original reverser arrangement in 1950. 5 April 1961. (Alan Dixon/Paul Watson)

From Birchencliffe, the route ran into Huddersfield along Halifax Road, through the pleasant suburb of Edgerton. This scene is at the Imperial Road stop, where no. 621 is seen on its way into town. The shelter on the right dates from the early 1900s and was one of several that survived around the trolleybus system in the 1960s. This one still survives today and is a listed structure. The road surface in the foreground has worn away to reveal the site of the tram track loop. Note the absence of other road traffic on this main road. 28 October 1961. (Alan Dixon/Paul Watson)

Marsden

Converted from trams	10 April 1938
Route length	7½ miles
Service linked to	Bradley
Closed to trolleybuses	30 January 1963
Last vehicle over whole route	560

Marsden terminus was at Fall Lane, just off the main A62 trunk road which the route followed from Huddersfield. Seen here, having just arrived and before turning, is no. 602. At the time that this photograph was taken (mid-1950s), this vehicle was one of the last to retain the 'Huddersfield Corporation' lettering on the cream waistband. (Jim Copland/Malcolm King collection)

At the terminus stop in the severe wintry conditions of early 1963 is no. 606, covered in road dirt. 27 January 1963. (Geoffrey Smith)

This view looks towards the main road, with the rural Pennine scenery typical of this route evident in the background. No. 622 stands at the terminus. 5 September 1962. (Tony Belton)

The last journey along the Colne Valley to Marsden was operated by no. 560. Here it waits at the terminus before returning to Longroyd Bridge depot. 30 January 1963. (Alan Dixon/Paul Watson)

The sub-zero temperatures can almost be felt in this view of no. 625, seen turning out of Fall Lane onto the A62. There was no heating for the crew or passengers on the trolleys. 27 January 1963. (Geoffrey Smith)

In much more pleasant weather, no. 604 makes the turn into Fall Lane with Marsden Parish Church in the background. 6 October 1962. (Alan Dixon/Paul Watson)

On the A62 road, entering Marsden is no. 551. It is negotiating roadworks, followed by heavy lorries on their way across the Pennines into Lancashire. Nowadays they use the M62 motorway across the moors to the west. 5 September 1962. (Tony Belton)

The most scenic part of the route was between Marsden and Slaithwaite, where wide panoramas opened up across the Colne Valley. No. 562 travels towards Slaithwaite. The wiring along the A62 was suspended towards the middle of the road to allow the faster trolleybuses to overtake slow moving lorries. (Stanley King – colour added by Malcolm Fraser)

Just further along this section was the turning circle for trolleys terminating at Slaithwaite (route no. 41). This was at Birks Well, where the circle area was scooped out of the hillside. This pleasant scene shows no. 541 waiting before returning to town. 6 October 1962. (Alan Dixon/Paul Watson)

Two Karrier trolleybuses are seen at the Birks Well turning point. On the right, no. 568 is in the circle waiting to depart for Bradley Leeds Road, whilst no. 492 is just setting off from the stop on the main road en route to Marsden. 7 September 1962. (Tony Belton)

The main trolleybus stop at Slaithwaite was at the Star Inn. Here, no. 611, setting off from the stop, passes no. 613. This view shows the Huddersfield style of designating trolleybus stopping places – a yellow band on a traction pole lettered 'Trolley Bus Stop'. 7 September 1962. (Tony Belton)

Near Cowlersley, the positive trolley pole of no. 559 has dewired, and has sustained considerable damage, possibly caused by hitting a traction pole. The passengers watch the attempts by the crew to retrieve the errant pole whilst waiting for the next trolley to take them into town. 1 June 1957. (Jim Copland/Malcolm King)

Longroyd Bridge Depot

Longroyd Bridge depot was the operating base of the trolleybus fleet. Built in 1938-9, and incorporating part of the tram depot here, it housed the entire trolleybus fleet, a maximum of 140 vehicles. Seen leaving the depot is no. 631, and in the entrance doorway is one of the 1949 AEC Mantador 'derricks', as the Huddersfield tower wagons were normally called. 6 July 1967. (David Clarke)

Leaving the depot, and about to turn right onto Manchester Road is no. 590. The presence of a considerable load of passengers on the vehicle is interesting – it is known that at tea-time and Saturday dinnertimes, workers at Brook Motors works in St Thomas Road would board a trolley about to enter service in the depot forecourt. This 'Football Ground' working could possibly be a journey from Canker Lane (on Leeds Road) to pick up mill workers. The wiring leading to the depot entrance, crossing the exit wires, is the direct link into the depot from the Marsden and Crosland Hill routes, and this was taken down in February 1964 after the closure of the latter service. 28 August 1963. (Tony Belton)

This scene is near the junction with Longroyd Lane, where the Longwood route branched off. No. 609 has just left the depot to take up service, and is being passed by no. 623 bound for Slaithwaite. 7 September 1962. (Tony Belton)

Crosland Hill

Converted from trams	3 October 1937
Route length	2½ miles
Service linked to	Birkby
Closed to trolleybuses	5 February 1964
Last vehicle over whole route	541

The turning circle at Crosland Hill was at the junction of Blackmoorfoot Road and Crosland Hill Road. It was on the edge of moorland and there were stone quarries in the vicinity, hence the cranes in the background. There was also the Standard Fireworks factory here. No. 621 and no. 596 stand in the circle. (Hugh Taylor)

A portrait of no. 549 standing at Crosland Hill terminus. This vehicle was one of the type never rebuilt, receiving a modified destination indicator layout in 1961. 28 August 1963. (Tony Belton)

Just below the Crosland Moor reverser at Dryclough Road, the gradient became severe enough to require the compulsory use of the coasting brake on descending journeys. Approaching this point (at Frederick Street) on a town-bound trolley, the photographer has captured this view of no. 603 climbing Blackmoorfoot Road to the terminus. 28 August 1963. (Tony Belton)

At Thornton Lodge, no. 596, passing no. 589, approaches the 'Griffin' junction where the Marsden route formerly branched off along Manchester Road (to the right). The wiring of the Thornton Lodge short-working turning circle is evident. This trolley retained its original dipped mudguards over the rear wheels (just visible) far longer than most of this type, losing them when overhauled in 1964. (Hugh Taylor)

Birkby

Converted from trams	7 November 1937
Route length	1½ miles
Service linked to	Crosland Hill
Closed to trolleybuses	5 February 1964
Last vehicle over whole route	544

This route was one of the shortest on the system and it served the dense housing of the Birkby area. The terminus was actually in the district of Fartown, and there was a wiring link from Fartown Bar on Bradford Road. This was used regularly by trolleys on Sunday mornings and late at night, when the Brackenhall service (route 10) was diverted via the Birkby route instead of its normal route direct into town via Bradford Road. This view at Fartown Bar on Boxing Day 1961 (when a Sunday service operated) shows no. 550 which is turning off Bradford Road into Spaines Road. Note the destination display showing 'Lockwood via Birkby'. Similar vehicle no. 577 is in the background working on the 90 route from Fixby. 26 December 1961. (Alan Dixon/Paul Watson)

The normal Birkby trolley service used a 'round the houses' terminal loop off Spaines Road. No. 639 is seen here turning into Woodbine Road with Fartown Bar visible in the background. Diverted route 10 journeys did not use this turning loop, and remained on Spaines Road using the wires in the centre upper foreground. There was a wiring connection from the Fartown Bar direction into Woodbine Road, this being used once daily on schooldays by the Bradley Bar to Salendine Nook Schools special journey which ran via Birkby. (Hugh Taylor)

The Birkby terminal stop was in Woodbine Road, where no. 574 is seen. This view dates from around 1959. Note the vehicle has black wheels. (H. Luff/Online Transport Archive)

A later view of the Birkby terminus showing no. 589 at the terminus. Note that that the metal shelter in the previous photograph has now been replaced by a concrete structure. Another trolley can be seen turning from Spaines Road in the background. (Hugh Taylor)

From Woodbine Road, the route turned right into Cobcroft Road, and then right again into Wasp Nest Road. No.639 has just left the terminus, and is about to make the turn into Cobcroft Road. Behind the wall at the far side of the vehicle is a railway cutting, carrying the goods-only branch to Newtown Goods Yard on St John's Road. (Hugh Taylor)

Alongside Spaines Road was the Fartown ground of Huddersfield Cricket and Athletic Club, and the home of the town's Rugby League side. Whilst the match was in progress, football special trolleys were parked in Spaines Road with poles down, to allow service trolleys to pass. Seen at the head of this line-up in Spaines Road is no. 577, which has a wooden chock placed behind its offside front wheel. The large building in the right background is Fartown Trinity Methodist Sunday School, which the author attended in his childhood, and later the associated Youth Group. The church itself was situated in Wasp Nest Road. 28 August 1963. (Tony Belton)

Almondbury

Converted from trams	4 December 1933
Route length	2 miles
Service linked to	West Vale until 1961, then Fixby from 1963
Closed to trolleybuses	14 July 1965
Last vehicle over whole route	593

The Almondbury route was the first in the town to be trolleybus operated. The terminus after 1950 was at a neat turning circle in Northgate, this replacing the reverser at Wormald Street. No. 584 is arriving on a through journey from Fixby. 29 August 1964. (David Pearson)

No. 634 is seen negotiating the turning circle, having arrived from West Vale. The buildings behind the vehicle are being demolished and a parade of shops would be built on the site. 13 May 1961. (Alan Dixon/Paul Watson)

Standing in the turning circle is no. 553, during the period between 1961 and 1963 when all journeys on this route operated as no.33 to the town only. The unpainted opening window frames at the upper deck front were a unique feature of this vehicle. Almondbury Parish Church stands on the left. The tranquility of this scene will be shattered after 4 o'clock when the local grammar school boys fight for a seat for their journey home. 5 September 1962. (Tony Belton)

No. 612 is loading passengers in Northgate, before descending towards town along Somerset Road. Town End is on the right and Highlands Avenue on the left. 10 July 1965. (Author)

Seen from the top deck of a passing trolley, no. 555 pauses in Somerset Road at the Longley Road stop. (Fred Ivey)

At the foot of Somerset Road, no. 639 is seen at Dog Kennel Bank, which goes off to the right. As can be seen, this was another location where a passenger shelter dating back to the early tram era was provided. 9 July 1965. (Tony Belton)

Trolleybus operation at the junction of Somerset Road and Wakefield Road whilst road widening works were in progress involved several overhead wiring alterations. These were to allow trolleys to take whichever path was available to traffic at the time. No. 579 is negotiating the works as it enters Somerset Road. Note the difference in levels of the carriageways and the fixed frog to allow alternative wiring paths to be taken. (Fred Ivey)

Evidence of the changes to the overhead alignments is evident in this view of no. 555 approaching the Wakefield Road junction. As can be seen, at this stage of the works, the carriageways were at different levels. (Fred Ivey)

Fixby

Converted from trams .... 30 June 1940 (part of Brighouse route)
Section closed beyond Fixby .... 9 July 1955
Route length .... 2½ miles
Service linked to .... Lockwood (1942-7), Longwood (1947-63), then Almondbury
Closed to trolleybuses .... 14 July 1965
Last vehicle over whole route 603

This route operated to a very affluent area of the town, and by 1960 the off-peak service frequency was every ½ hour, well below the level for efficient trolleybus operation. The terminus, seen here, was at the junction of Fixby Road and Lightridge Road and before 1955 the route continued across the Borough Boundary to the left of view. No. 580 has reversed into the latter road, and is about to pull forward to the terminal stop. After January 1963, this was route 34 through to Almondbury. July 1964.
(E.C. Bennett/Online Transport Archive)

Standing at the terminal stop is no. 596, when the route was no. 90 to Longwood. The black-painted wheels indicate that this is a late-1950s view, red painted wheels being introduced during 1959.
(H. Luff/Online Transport Archive)

The Brighouse trams ran across the fields on reserved tracks between Fixby and Smithy, but the trolleys had to take a slightly longer route via Bradley Bar, where the main Bradford Road was reached. Here, no. 624 is seen turning into Fixby Road. 9 July 1965. (Author)

At Bradley Bar there was a short working turning loop at the roundabout which was designated route no. 93. This had been little used until 1960, when the All Saints Catholic Secondary School was opened nearby. From then, several trolleys ran school specials in the morning and afternoon. No. 596, seen in its final state after overhaul in 1964, waits for pupils ahead of similar vehicle no. 605. Note the unconnected frog assembly in the wiring – this was erected in 1964 to allow a complete circle of wiring around the island which was never completed. 28 May 1965. (Tony Belton)

From Bradley Bar towards the town centre, there was a stretch of dual carriageway which had been completed just before the Second World War. This ended at Longhill Road, where no. 627 is seen picking up passengers. 13 May 1965. (David Clarke)

Seen approaching the 'New Inn' (later known as the 'Ashbrow') is no. 602 climbing towards Bradley Bar. The reserved sleeper-track tramway for the Brighouse trams started behind the 'New Inn' and trams turned into Netheroyd Hill Road which is in the right background. Bradford Road is now a dual-carriageway from Bradley Bar to Fartown Bar. 9 July 1965. (Author)

Brackenhall

Converted from trams	19 June 1938 (as Sheepridge route)
Extended to Brackenhall	6 March 1949
Route length	2½ miles
Service linked to	Longwood until 1947, then Lockwood
Closed to trolleybuses	13 July 1966
Last vehicle over whole route	629

The Brackenhall route served a large council housing estate. Originally the route ran to Sheepridge (Ashbrow Road) and was linked as a circular service with the Woodhouse route, which in turn was extended to Riddings. The main road in Brackenhall is Bradley Boulevard, and the trolleys ran along its length, terminating in a turning circle at its northern end. Here no. 590 is seen before departing for Lockwood. 28 August 1963. (Tony Belton)

No. 548 is seen in Bradley Boulevard having just departed from the terminus, which can be seen in the background. September 1965. (David Pearson)

Trolleys reached Brackenhall from Bradford Road via a reverse curve in Ashbrow Road. No. 554 unloads passengers at Smithy, before tackling the curve and climbing to Brackenhall. Note the tram shelter on the right, which was removed shortly after this photograph was taken. 19 May 1964. (Roland Box)

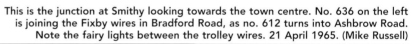

This is the junction at Smithy looking towards the town centre. No. 636 on the left is joining the Fixby wires in Bradford Road, as no. 612 turns into Ashbrow Road. Note the fairy lights between the trolley wires. 21 April 1965. (Mike Russell)

Bradford Road (Brackenhall and Fixby routes)

Between Smithy and Fartown Bar there was only one trolley stop – this being at Dewhurst Road. During his teenage years, the author lived just off Bradford Road and this was his nearest stop to travel into town and on schooldays through to Almondbury. On the last day of trolley operation of the Brackenhall route, passengers board no. 627 in the morning rush hour. Overtaking is a Joint Omnibus Committee AEC Regent V motorbus heading to town on the route from Bailiff Bridge via Brighouse – the service that effectively replaced the trolleys between Fixby and Brighouse. Note that the Corporation trolleys and the JOC motorbuses had separate bus stops and higher fares applied on the latter services over common sections of route. 13 July 1966. (Author)

Another 'last day' shot shows no. 602 departing from the Dewhurst Road stop heading towards Smithy and Brackenhall in the late afternoon. 13 July 1966. (Author)

On a bright Spring day in 1965, no. 590 is seen approaching the Dewhurst Road stop from the Fartown Bar direction. It is working a school special journey to Bradley Bar. This photograph was taken just after 8 o'clock in the morning from the upper deck front seat of an Almondbury-bound trolleybus. (Bas Longbottom)

Riddings

Opened	19 June 1938 (as Woodhouse route)
Extended to Riddings	6 March 1949
Route length	2½ miles
Service linked to	Newsome
Closed to trolleybuses	13 July 1966
Last vehicle over whole route	600

This route was never tram operated, and was originally linked as a circular service with the Sheepridge route. Riddings was another large council housing estate and the terminus was at a turning circle approximately half-way along Riddings Road where no. 565 is seen. 28 August 1963. (Tony Belton)

The main feature of the Riddings route was Woodhouse Hill, which rose sharply from Fartown Green to Woodhouse, being a gradient of 1 in 8½ at its steepest point. No. 579 is seen near the top of the climb. Before 1949 trolleys turned into Ashbrow Road (on the right), and returned to town via Sheepridge. When the two routes were separated, the wiring along this part of Ashbrow Road was dismantled. 21 April 1965. (Mike Russell)

Trolleys ran down Woodhouse Hill using the coasting-brake. No. 629 is seen approaching the only stop on the descent at Central Avenue. 8 July 1966. (David Clarke)

No. 610 is seen at the foot of the hill, and will shortly come to a halt to allow the coasting-brake to be disengaged. There was a turning circle at this point known as 'Fartown Green', and it was used when snow and ice prevented trolleys using Woodhouse Hill. 9 July 1966. (Author)

Looking in the opposite direction to the previous photograph, this view shows the turning circle around the small park area on the right. No. 597 pauses at the stop before tackling Woodhouse Hill, which will be achieved with ease. This vehicle together with no 596, retained chrome windscreen surrounds until withdrawal. 1 July 1966. (Mike Russell)

In the 1960s there were no scheduled turns at the Fartown Green circle (although one tea-time special did turn here on weekdays in the 1950s). The photographer was extremely lucky to record no. 546 using the circle on driver training duties shortly before the Riddings route was converted to motorbuses. 1 July 1966. (Mike Russell)

From Woodhouse Hill, the route ran along Fartown Green Road to Fartown Bar. No. 606 is approaching Fartown Bar with Woodhouse Hill visible in the left background. Note that the trolleybus stop sign on the traction pole has been painted out and a bus stop plate erected in readiness for the introduction of motorbuses. 8 July 1966. (David Pearson)

Fartown Bar (Riddings, Brackenhall and Fixby Routes)

At Fartown Bar, the Riddings route turned onto Bradford Road, joining the Fixby and Brackenhall routes. After the demise of the Birkby route in 1964, this was a much simplified wiring junction. No. 600 is seen here turning from Bradford Road into Fartown Green Road. July 1964 (E.C. Bennett/Online Transport Archive).

No. 628 arrives at Fartown Bar from the Brackenhall direction. To the right is Fartown Green Road with the Royal Hotel on the corner. 8 July 1966 (David Pearson)

Seen at the southern end of Bradford Road, at the Alder Street junction, is no. 591 (with body from no. 561). The area in the background is known as Hillhouse. 19 May 1964. (Roland Box)

Bradford Road ends at its junction with Viaduct Street (on the left) and Northgate (on the right). Here, under the viaduct arch, the Brackenhall and Riddings routes turned into Viaduct Street, and (from 1963) the Fixby route ran into town via Northgate. Also at this point was the loop serving the Transport Department works at Great Northern Street, and the trailing frog of this can be seen at the upper right of this view. No. 638 is making the turn on to Viaduct Street. (Fred Ivey)

Great Northern Street Works

All major overhaul work on the trolleybus fleet was carried out in the works. A newly overhauled and repainted trolley was a sight to behold and the smell of varnish lingered for several weeks after the trolley re-entered service. The paintwork was expected to last for seven years, hence the thoroughness of the workmanship. In this view, no. 595 is seen inside the works following its overhaul in June 1964. (Hugh Taylor)

This view looks towards Leeds Road and shows the Gas Works train in action in Beaumont Street. Diesel haulage replaced steam locomotives in the 1960s and the railway ceased operation in 1966. The imposing frontage of the Great Northern Street works can be seen. The building dated from the steam tram era in 1887, but the frontage with multiple doorways dated from 1909. The open space on the left was used by the weekly 'Monday Market'. (Fred Ivey)

Lockwood

Converted from trams	12 January 1939
Route length	1½ miles
Service linked to	Brighouse (1942-7) then Sheepridge/ Brackenhall
Closed to trolleybuses	13 July 1966
Last vehicle over whole route	602

The turning circle at Lockwood was built on the hillside behind Lockwood Church, and accessed by a narrow road. In this view, a BUT vehicle is standing in the turning circle in Taylor Hill Road. (Author's collection)

This close-up of no. 634 standing in the turning circle shows how the vehicle is leaning over due to the hilly site. 24 June 1966. (Alan Murray-Rust)

No. 595 has turned off the main Woodhead Road (leading to Honley) as it approaches the terminus. Its destination indicator has already been set for the return journey. Note the forest of mill chimneys and church spires in the background. 24 June 1966. (Alan Murray-Rust)

Seen turning from Lockwood Road into Bridge Street at Lockwood Bar is trolley no. 554. (Hugh Taylor)

Newsome

Converted from trams	2 May 1937, (route extended to 'Newsome South')
Route length	2 miles
Service linked to	Woodhouse/Riddings
Closed to trolleybuses	13 July 1966
Last vehicle over whole route	600 (629 subsequently to Newsome Church)

The terminus at Newsome, described as 'Newsome South', was actually situated in Berry Brow. Here there was a triangular reverser at the junction of Newsome Road and Caldercliffe Road. No. 598 is seen in mid-reverse. In the background can be seen the Victoria Tower on Castle Hill, which dominates the Huddersfield skyline. The tower was completed in 1899, being erected to celebrate Queen Victoria's Diamond Jubilee of 1897. 2 July 1966. (Mike Russell)

Seen at the terminal stop in Caldercliffe Road is no. 588. In the background is the Berry Brow Infants School, where the author's mother taught in the late 1930s. One of her pupils was Derek Ibbotson, who went on to become an international athlete, winning a bronze medal at the 1956 Melbourne Olympic Games in the 5,000 metres event, and in 1957 holding the British record for the mile. (David Pearson)

Also at the terminus is no. 543 operating an enthusiast's tour for the Huddersfield Trolleybus Preservation Society on 17 April 1966. This body hoped to raise funds to purchase a trolleybus and was founded by three schoolfriends, (Bas Longbottom, David Beach and the author), all of whom are seen on the left of this view. The Transport Department kindly allowed the vehicle to display the destination blind from a Cleethorpes trolleybus for the occasion. (Carl Isgar)

After leaving the terminus, the trolleys climbed Newsome Road to the summit of the route at Newsome Church, where there was a triangular reverser. No. 629 is starting the descent towards the terminus, whilst the trolley in the background is about to tackle the even steeper descent towards the town. 2 July 1966. (Mike Russell)

The Newsome Church reverser was regularly used by a two-vehicle off-peak shuttle service to the town (route no. 21). No. 578 is seen in Church Street, having reversed and ready to move forward to the stop in Newsome Road. At the end of Church Street was Lockwood Scar, a very steep road that led down to Lockwood. (Fred Ivey)

From Newsome Church, trolleys faced the severely graded Newsome Road, which dropped down to river level. The gradient was severe enough for the coasting-brake to be used for part of this section. This was applied at the Dawson Road stop, and for the last couple of years or so of trolleybus operation, a red 'Coasting Brake' sign was attached to the stop plate here (with a corresponding green plate at the end of the section at Stile Common). No. 605 pauses at Dawson Road for the brake to be engaged. 8 July 1966. (David Pearson)

There was one intermediate stop along the coasting-brake section and this was at Tunnacliffe Road, where no. 599 is seen with the panorama of the town in the background. (E.C. Bennett/Online Transport Archive)

After 1949, the end of the coasting brake section was at Stile Common, where no. 557 is seen. Note the tram shelter on the left. 8 July 1961. (Alan Dixon/Paul Watson)

At the western end of Colne Road, the Newsome wires met those from Lockwood at the foot of Chapel Hill. This was another steep hill, leading to the town centre, but was relatively short in length. Having operated the automatic frog, no. 625 is seen turning into Colne Road with Chapel Hill in the background. 22 April 1965. (Mike Russell)

Chapel Hill (Newsome and Lockwood routes)

The revised arrangement at Chapel Hill after road improvements in 1961 is seen here, the new road veering to the right of the old alignment. No. 635 is preceding no. 604 up the hill into the town centre. This scene was painted by L.S. Lowry in 1965 in his distinctive style, but he did not include any trolleybus wiring. The work, entitled 'Huddersfield', is displayed in the town's art gallery. 15 June 1966. (Marcus Eavis/Online Transport Archive)

Bradley

Converted from trams	19 June 1938
Route length	3 miles
Keldregate extension opened	2 April 1956
Service linked to	Marsden until 1963, then Longwood
Closed to trolleybuses	12 July 1967
Last vehicle over whole route	624 (Keldregate), (620 last to Leeds Road)

The Keldregate terminus at Bradley was the last significant extension to the trolleybus system and served new housing. The turning circle was within the wide junction of Keldregate and Bradley Road. This wide view taken from Bradley Road shows no. 640 standing at the terminal stop. (Carl Isgar)

No. 621 comes around the turning circle at Keldregate before picking up the waiting passengers. 17 June 1967. (Mike Russell)

Trolleys reached Keldregate from Leeds Road via Brooklands. No. 620 is seen negotiating the sharp bend as it turns from Brooklands into Keldregate. The 'Little John' public house is on the right. 3 April 1967. (David Pearson)

At the junction with Leeds Road (the main A62 trunk road), Brooklands is split into two carriageways around a green. No. 629, having negotiated the trigger-operated frog on Leeds Road, is turning into the part of Brooklands where the two carriageways join. In the background can be seen the abandoned viaduct of the ill-fated Midland Railway branch from Mirfield which terminated at the Newtown Goods Yard in Huddersfield. 12 July 1967. (Alan Dixon/Paul Watson)

The original Bradley terminus (designated Leeds Road, after 1956) was at the junction with Bradley Road, near Cooper Bridge and just within the Borough boundary. No. 583 is seen completing the turn at the wide road junction. 28 August 1963. (Tony Belton)

This bleak view of the Brooklands junction shows no. 546, which has come from Keldregate, turning onto Leeds Road whilst no. 565 waits to proceed towards the Leeds Road terminus. 21 February 1963. (Tony Belton)

The Bradley route had several short-working turning points along its length, this one being at the foot of Deighton Road where a reversing triangle was situated. Special journeys (designated route 44) worked to here for workpeople at the nearby LB Holliday chemical works. No. 616 is seen having reversed from Leeds Road, prior to turning back towards the town centre. 21 April 1965. (Mike Russell)

No. 604 is seen turning into Leeds Road from Deighton Road after using the reversing triangle. 27 March 1962. (Alan Dixon/Paul Watson)

This scene showing the Deighton reverser looks towards the town centre and shows no. 615 setting down passengers before proceeding to the Leeds Road terminus. Just to the left of this vehicle can be seen another trolley which is crossing the bridge over the main railway between Huddersfield and Leeds. This view was taken on the last day of trolleybus operation on the route. 12 July 1967. (David Clarke)

After crossing the main line railway, Leeds Road drops down to pass under the former Kirkburton branch railway. Here no. 638 is about to negotiate the bridge on its way towards the town centre. 6 July 1967. (David Clarke)

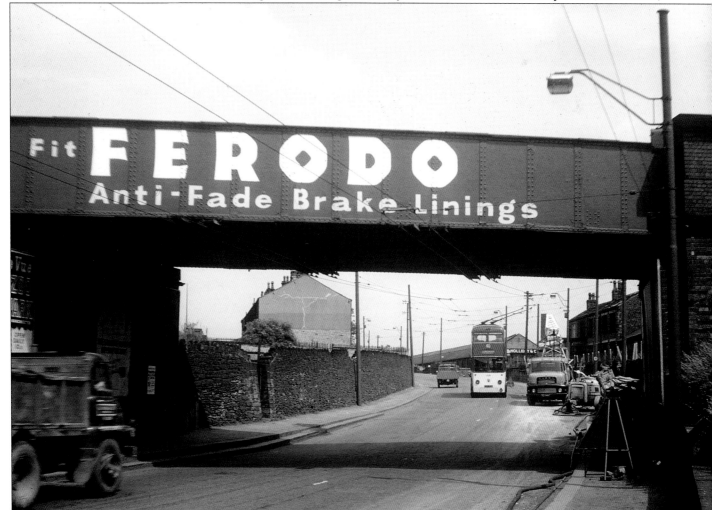

At the large ICI plant (known until the later 1940s as 'British Dyes'), there was a turning loop around Woodlands Road and Ashgrove Road for specials (designated route 42) to turn. No. 613 is seen entering the loop from Leeds Road, and is about to pass coaches from the Hanson and the associated Bottomley fleets. Hanson's had a haulage depot here. The loop was tree-lined and had a semi-rural aspect. In the far background, across the valley is the Riddings housing estate. 18 June 1967. (Mike Russell)

The ICI works was at the town end of the loop, just before trolleys turned back onto Leeds Road. Here no. 519 is loading passengers on a through journey to Newsome South. Until 1959, when the road here was realigned, the loop passed along to the right behind the queue. 18 May 1961. (David Clarke)

Trolleybuses gather at the ICI works loading stop. No. 577, which is about to turn onto Leeds Road, has evidently manoeuvred past no. 573, whose trolleys are being replaced on the overhead. No. 636 is in the background. (Hugh Taylor)

Further along Leeds Road towards the town was the Leeds Road ground of Huddersfield Town Football Club. There were two turning facilities for trolleybuses here, this one being at Canker Lane, where a turning circle was provided on unpaved ground. No. 624 is seen pausing at the stop here before proceeding towards Bradley. 16 June 1967. (Mike Russell)

The approach to the town centre along Leeds Road, is very industrial, being bordered by mills, factories as well as the electricity generating station (which supplied the power for the trolleybus system) and the gasworks. No. 636, Bradley-bound, is passing the junction with Hillhouse Lane, a scene which today is almost unrecognisable. Only the 'Slaters Arms' on the left survives, and it faces the multi-lane A62 highway. 12 July 1967. (David Clarke)

After the road reconstruction of the early 1960s, the town end of Leeds Road became a dual carriageway as it approached the new ring road at Northumberland Street roundabout. No. 627 is seen here about to turn onto the roundabout. In the background is a Yorkshire Woollen District bus, and in the far left can be seen the electricity works cooling towers and the gas works gas holder. 17 June 1967. (Mike Russell)

Longwood

Converted from trams   1 January 1939
Route length   3 miles
Service linked to   Sheepridge until 1947, Brighouse/Fixby (1947-63), then Bradley
Closed to trolleybuses   12 July 1967
Last vehicle over whole route   636

During the harsh winter of 1963, snow lays on the rooftops in this image of Longwood terminus. No. 622 is about to reverse on to the turntable platform. 21 February 1963.

Trolley no. 569 at a wintry Longwood terminus. 21 February 1963. (Tony Belton)

No. 583 reverses onto the turntable under the guidance of the conductor who is following the correct procedure. There was not much clearance here and drivers had to be careful to avoid grounding the platform of the vehicle. The road leading off to the right is Gilead Road, which led to Longwood Edge and the Outlane route. 3 April 1967. (David Pearson)

A view across the valley, showing no. 570 standing on the turntable platform before moving forward to reach the terminal stop. (Fred Ivey)

Rollover

There were only two instances of Huddersfield trolleybuses accidentally overturning. The first occurred at Leeches Hill, Outlane on 4th October 1938, where no. 12, which had a brake defect, left the road and overturned in high winds (See page 188). The other incident happened in 1967 at Longwood terminus, as depicted here. Fortunately, neither incident resulted in any significant human casualties.

This remarkable event took place on Monday 13 February 1967, just months before trolleybus operation ceased. At 7.30am, the driver of no. 634 mis-judged the reversing movement, and the vehicle crashed through the railings and fell into the field below, overturning in the process. Fortunately, apart from the trolley, there were no severe injuries. This was the scene later that morning as local youngsters (it was the half-term holiday) survey the damage. Note there were no high-vis jackets or barriers keeping the public away in those days. The Transport Department pole-crane was used to remove the traction motor from the trolley. (Dave Hill/David Pearson)

The rear of no. 634 lay in the field below the turntable platform. Prior to being recovered, the trolley gear was removed as well as the traction motor. In 1965, this vehicle had been the last trolley to receive a full repaint. 13 February 1967. (Dave Hill/David Pearson)

The recovery of the vehicle took place on the following day. To enable this, the overhead wiring leading to the reverser was temporarily dismantled, and the trees around the site were severely pruned. (Nicholas Harris/Don Akrigg)

This is the dramatic moment when no. 634 was suspended in mid-air before being set down upright onto its own wheels. It was towed back to Longroyd Bridge Depot from where it was subsequently sold for scrap. (Nicholas Harris/Don Akrigg)

Standing at the Longwood terminal stop is no. 541 which is waiting to depart for St George's Square only. The mis-match of the basic off-peak frequencies of the no. 90 Longwood service (every 15 minutes) and the Fixby service (every 30 minutes) meant every other departure from here being to the town centre only. To the right, above the vehicle, is an example of a weaver's house. Before industrialisation of the woollen industry, cloth weaving was done by home workers with a hand loom situated in the upper floor, which is why there were multiple windows allowing as much daylight as possible into the weaving room. 14 January 1961. (Alan Dixon/Paul Watson)

This is another view in Longwood Gate, showing no. 588 passing Joseph Hoyle's Prospect Mill, which has since been demolished. (Fred Ivey)

The main street in Longwood clung to the valley side and was quite narrow, often being cited as the reason why the town's trolleys were all built to the narrow width of 7 feet 6 inches. In this view, no. 627 is in Longwood Gate as it nears the terminus. Note the double bracket arm suspension for the wiring – this avoided planting traction poles on both sides of the narrow road. 17 June 1967. (Mike Russell)

A pleasant scene as no. 612 passes the War Memorial in Longwood Gate en route to the terminus. (David Pearson)

Leaving Longwood village, the route dropped down sharply to negotiate a hairpin bend at Quarmby Clough. No. 638 is seen at the sharp bend, with Hoyle's Quarmby Clough Mills on the right. 5 September 1962. (Tony Belton)

The road still clung to the valley side here, and in this scene no. 625 is accelerating away from Quarmby Clough towards Paddock on a service 90 journey to St George's Square. 14 January 1961. (Alan Dixon/Paul Watson)

On this part of the route there were wide views visible across the Colne Valley. Here, no. 592 approaches Quarmby Clough from the Paddock direction, with a view of Milnsbridge railway viaduct (on the main line to Manchester), and Crosland Hill in the far background. No. 592 was the last trolley to be rebodied, receiving the body from no. 563 in late 1963.
21 April 1965.
(Mike Russell)

Further towards the town centre, no. 617 is in Longwood Road about to pass a Ford Prefect car. In the background can be seen the housing at Leymoor, and on the horizon is Scapegoat Hill. Both these areas were served by Joint Omnibus Committee buses. 17 June 1967. (Mike Russell)

At the very wide junction of Longwood Road and Quarmby Road was the
Paddock short working turning circle which was regularly used during weekdays.
The circle was moved from Paddock Head to this point in 1959. No. 593, in its
short-lived guise following overhaul in 1964, is seen waiting to depart on a
journey to Bradley Leeds Road. In the background is a Hanson's AEC single deck
bus on the suburban Lindley to Newsome route. 21 April 1965. (Mike Russell)

In the mid-1960s, the road space at the junction was partly filled
by an elongated island. This is evident in this view of no. 614 in
the turning loop. To the left is no. 626 passing the circle on a
journey from Longwood. 12 July 1967. (David Clarke)

No. 563 emerges from Church Street and is about to negotiate the Paddock Head roundabout. Until 1959, when the roundabout was installed, the Paddock turning circle was situated at this point. 5 September 1962. (Tony Belton)

At The Triangle, a series of bends took the route into Longroyd Bridge. No. 614 comes round the curve from Market Street. 16 June 1967. (Mike Russell)

Looking in the opposite direction to the previous view, no. 620 has just negotiated the 'S' bend from Longroyd Lane, passing under the Paddock railway viaduct, which carries the line to Sheffield. (Alan Dixon / Paul Watson)

After passing under Paddock Viaduct, the route ran along Longroyd Lane to Longroyd Bridge. Behind the wall on the left was the Huddersfield Narrow Canal. In the pouring rain, no. 598 overtakes a parked Ford Prefect car. This was another very narrow part of the route where double bracket arms were used. (David Pearson)

The Longwood route joined the Crosland Hill and Marsden wires at the junction of Longroyd Lane and Manchester Road. In this busy scene, no. 529 is crossing into Longroyd Lane. 7 September 1962. (Tony Belton)

At Longroyd Bridge, no. 613 is seen approaching the advanced turnout for the Longwood route before stopping to pick up a passenger. It has slowed to activate the automatic frog, allowing a Morris Minor car to overtake. St Thomas' Church is in the background. 16 June 1967. (Mike Russell)

As it approaches the town centre, no. 614 is passing the junction with Outcote Bank. Until March 1964, when the town centre reconstruction work caused the route to be abandoned, inbound trolleys from Longroyd Bridge ran up Outcote Bank, the direct wires to Chapel Hill only being used by trolleys entering service from the depot. 16 June 1967. (Mike Russell)

Waterloo

Converted from trams	11 November 1934
Route length	2½ miles
Service linked to	Lindley (71) or Outlane (73)
Closed to trolleybuses	13 July 1968
Last vehicle over whole route	629 (623 subsequently as civic special)

The district of Waterloo was named after the Waterloo Bridge, built in 1819 carrying the new turnpike road towards Wakefield. The Waterloo public house stands at the junction of the Penistone and Wakefield Roads. Trolleys turned here by way of a 'round the houses' loop. The pub is in the background of this view as no. 622 turns from Wakefield Road into Penistone Road at the start of the one-way circuit. 14 June 1968. (David Clarke)

No. 637 is turning off Penistone Road to climb Mitchell Avenue. In the background a blue and white County Motors bus can be seen leaving its depot. 14 June 1968. (David Clarke)

The terminal stop was near the top of Mitchell Avenue where rebuild no. 585 is seen. The East Lancashire body on this vehicle was the last new trolleybus body built in Britain on a six-wheel chassis. It entered service in this form in the Spring of 1962. 9 June 1966. (Marcus Eavis/Online Transport Archive)

After departing from the terminus in Mitchell Avenue, trolleys ran down Waterloo Rise to rejoin Wakefield Road opposite the Waterloo, where no. 626 is seen making the turn. 6 July 1968. (Mike Russell)

On its way into town, no. 620 is seen passing Ravensknowle Park, a quiet haven in contrast to the very busy traffic along Wakefield Road. 10 July 1967. (David Clarke)

Near to Moldgreen, no. 629 pauses to pick up passengers opposite
Grosvenor Road. Here the Moldgreen loop wires emerged and trailed into
the Wakefield Road route just behind the trolley. 1 June 1968. (John Laker)

This scene is at the Moldgreen junction, and the wires of the one-way Moldgreen loop are
evident on the right turning into Broad Lane. No. 587 is staying on Wakefield Road en route
to Waterloo. This vehicle carries the body from no. 557. 22 April 1965. (Mike Russell)

From Broad Lane, the Moldgreen loop turned into Grand Cross Road, where no. 628 is seen whilst operating an enthusiasts' tour on the last Sunday of trolleybus operation. From here the loop turned into Grosvenor Road, shortly before turning back into Wakefield Road. 7 July 1968. (Mike Russell)

From Moldgreen, the route descended to the Somerset Road 'Lyceum' junction of the Almondbury route. As already mentioned in the Almondbury route section, this junction was totally rebuilt in 1964/5. This view looking towards the town dates from just before the works started, and shows, on the left, no. 591, and on the right no. 596 which is heading for Waterloo. Between them is a JOC AEC Regent motorbus on the Lowerhouses service which like the Almondbury trolleys, turned into Somerset Road at this point. In the early 1930s, the Lowerhouses service was planned to be the first experimental trolleybus route. 13 June 1964. (Alan Dixon/Paul Watson)

Shortly after the Somerset Road junction, Wakefield Road crosses Somerset Bridge over the River Colne at Aspley. In this view a BUT trolley is crossing the bridge on its way into town. The structure was subsequently rebuilt to carry the widened road in the mid-1960s. 13 June 1964. (Alan Dixon/Paul Watson)

Lindley

Converted from trams	11 November 1934
Route length	2½ miles
Service linked to	Waterloo
Closed to trolleybuses	13 July 1968
Last vehicle over whole route	638

At Lindley, trolleys turned by means of a 'round the houses' loop. No. 571 is turning from Lidget Street into Thomas Street at the start of the loop. 14 March 1961. (Alan Dixon/Paul Watson)

From Thomas Street, the loop turned into Thorncliffe Street, where no. 631 is seen passing a Hanson's AEC Regal bus. This would be laying-over before commencing a journey on the suburban route to Newsome. 15 June 1967. (Mike Russell)

The last part of the loop was in West Street, and no. 544 is seen here about to turn right into Lidget Street to reach the terminal stop. 7 September 1962. (Tony Belton)

The Lindley terminus was at a lay-by near the north end of Lidget Street, where passengers are boarding no. 571. Originally fitted with a front bumper, this vehicle has recently had it removed, resulting in a very short dash panel. 14 March 1961. (Alan Dixon/Paul Watson)

Another scene at the Lindley terminus shows no. 614 at the terminal stop with a Hanson's AEC Reliance bus waiting behind on the Newsome service. 'Via Quarmby' was a peak hour variant of the service. The bus was originally a coach, but was rebuilt and rebodied in 1966. It was to pass into the Corporation bus fleet when the Hanson's Buses operation was purchased in 1969. 24 June 1966. (Alan Murray-Rust)

A notable feature along the Lindley route was the Lindley Clock Tower, situated where Lidget Street becomes Acre Street. No. 622 stops here to pick up passengers on 1 June 1968. (John Laker)

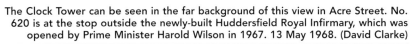

The Clock Tower can be seen in the far background of this view in Acre Street. No. 620 is at the stop outside the newly-built Huddersfield Royal Infirmary, which was opened by Prime Minister Harold Wilson in 1967. 13 May 1968. (David Clarke)

At Marsh, there was a turning loop for trolleys working on route 72, which before 1965 had a regular weekday service across town to Moldgreen. Seen here turning from Acre Street into Wellington Street at the start of the loop is no. 584. 1 June 1967. (David Pearson)

At the southern end of Acre Street was the Bay Horse junction with New Hey Road, and the Outlane wires. No. 639 is about to turn into Westbourne Road on its way into town. This vehicle was the last trolley to be given an overhaul, and in true Huddersfield fashion, it re-entered service in June 1966 with a new 'face'. Its registration plate was mounted on the towing hatch and thus became instantly recognisable to local trolleybus aficionados. 1 June 1968. (John Laker)

The Bay Horse public house is in the background to this view of no.619 joining the Outlane route wires. New Hey Road, in the background, was widened as a dual carriageway in the mid-1960s. This vehicle is in a short-lived condition with no front bumper but retaining semaphore trafficators. The more modern winking variety was fitted when it was overhauled in 1963. 7 September 1962. (Tony Belton)

Outlane

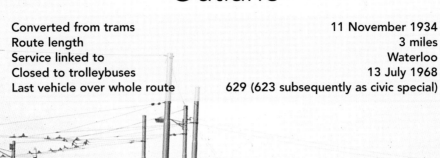

Converted from trams	11 November 1934
Route length	3 miles
Service linked to	Waterloo
Closed to trolleybuses	13 July 1968
Last vehicle over whole route	629 (623 subsequently as civic special)

The village of Outlane was situated on the very edge of Pennine moorland to the west of Huddersfield. The trolleybus terminus was at the west end of the village, 909 feet above sea level. No. 640 is seen at the terminus lay-by, with a view looking across to Longwood Edge. 6 July 1968. (Mike Russell)

In winter, this area was more prone to severe weather – if it was raining in Huddersfield it might well be snowing at Outlane. No. 576 stands in the terminal lay-by during the bleak winter of 1963, when snow lay on the ground for several weeks. 21 February 1963. (Tony Belton)

The terminal stop was at the other side of the road from the lay-by. No. 605 is seen here crossing New Hey Road. 24 June 1966. (Alan Murray-Rust)

No. 622 stands in the sunshine at the terminal stop, whilst a derrick attends to the overhead at the turning circle, probably as a result of an earlier dewirement. New Hey Road continues across the moors into Lancashire and a JOC bus service operated along here as far as Nont Sarah's, a popular hostelry. 5 September 1962. (Tony Belton)

In the middle of the village was the junction with Stainland Road, which was the original tram terminus (steam and later electric) and a tram waiting shelter was provided. This point was also the terminus of a bus route from Halifax. In this view no. 614 meets a Halifax Leyland bus, with the waiting shelter visible between them. Note that this one had an integral red police box, just visible by the nearside front of the trolley. (BTS Trolleyslides)

This panoramic view, taken on the last day of normal trolley operation, shows a BUT trolley climbing out of the village towards the summit of the route at Leeches Hill. In a couple of days the trolleys were gone, and in a few years, the green fields on the left were obliterated by the M62 motorway. 12 July 1968. (Mike Russell)

No. 603 reaches the summit at Leeches Hill en route to town. Lindley Moor Road goes off to the right. Today this area is junction 23 of the M62, with a roundabout and slip roads to and from the motorway. 11 June 1966. (Marcus Eavis/Online Transport Archive)

The area on the town side of the summit is known as Mount. In this rural scene, a Sunbeam S7 trolley is held up by a herd of cows crossing New Hey Road. 6 July 1968. (Mike Russell)

No. 625 is seen at Longwood Edge with Mount in the right background, and a hazy view across to Outlane on the left. As its name implies, Longwood Edge leads down to Longwood. 22 April 1965. (Mike Russell)

From Mount, it was almost a continual descent to the town centre. At Salendine Nook, near Raw Nook Road, there was a reversing triangle into a lane beside the Co-operative stores. This point was designated route 74, and it was regularly used by peak hour workings, many of these being through journeys to Moldgreen. Evidently no. 618, seen reversing, is working through to Waterloo on this occasion. 14 April 1965. (David Pearson)

No. 635 stands beside the Co-operative store before turning back into New Hey Road. 22 April 1965. (Mike Russell)

A short distance east of the Salendine Nook reverser was the loop constructed in 1957 for vehicles carrying schoolchildren to Salendine Nook Schools. This view shows trolleybuses gathering at the loop awaiting the afternoon school finishing time. No. 638 is seen turning off New Hey Road, followed by no. 567. On the far right is no. 614 at the loading point. 26 March 1962. (Alan Dixon / Paul Watson)

The wiring at the loop was constructed using span wires and curve segment assemblies. No. 568 comes round the loop followed by no. 593. 26 March 1962. (Alan Dixon/Paul Watson)

At the loading point, no. 503 is at the head of the queue, as pupils from the Girls' High School approach for their ride home. 26 March 1962. (Alan Dixon/Paul Watson)

No. 617 pulls out from the loop after dropping pupils at the school. The number of trolleys operating school specials reduced as the fleet contracted, and by the end in 1968 only one such journey was scheduled, this being the morning through trip from Waterloo. The new substation, which enabled the use of trolleybus specials to be stepped-up in 1960, can be seen in the left background behind the vehicle. New Hey Road stretches out into the distance towards Outlane. 15 June 1967. (Mike Russell)

This scene is in New Hey Road at Oakes, showing no. 501 working on a school special from Salendine Nook, approaching the Bay Horse junction at Marsh. It is passing under the trailing frog of the Marsh turning loop at Gibson Street. This part of New Hey Road was extensively rebuilt in the mid-1960s as shown in the following photographs. 26 March 1962. (Alan Dixon/Paul Watson)

The works in New Hey Road Oakes resulted in a dual carriageway road being provided from the Bay Horse junction to Tanyard Road. Lay-bys were provided at bus stops and wiring for the trolleys was erected on the new westbound carriageway. This scene shows no. 631 pulling into the stop at Oakes Road on the new formation. Wellington Mills dominates the background, and on the opposite side of the road is a 'just delivered' Daimler Fleetline motorbus on test, one of the type that replaced the trolleys in 1967-8. 16 June 1967. (Mike Russell)

No. 559 is in New Hey Road, about to join the wiring from Lindley at the Bay Horse junction. 7 September 1962. (Tony Belton)

At the Bay Horse, no. 543 is seen entering the new westbound carriageway en route for Outlane. The Lindley route wires go off to the right. Note the automatic frog indicator on the traction pole, which lit up when the frog for Lindley had been activated by the driver. In case this failed, there was a hand trigger and the pole is marked with the legend 'Operate for Acre Street'. 15 June 1967. (Mike Russell)

This scene looks south at the Bay Horse, looking towards Westbourne Road. No. 546, in its first week of service after receiving a new East Lancashire body, has just left the stop here, and passed through the wiring junction with the Lindley route. 14 March 1961. (Alan Dixon/Paul Watson)

Gledholt and Trinity Street (Outlane and Lindley routes)

Three trolleys are seen at Gledholt, near the western entrance to Greenhead Park. On the left, at the lay-by outside the Ambulance Station (out of view), no. 638 on route 72 leads no. 634 on route 71. Passing in the other direction is no. 574 en route to Lindley. In the background can be seen the Snodley reservoir at the top of Trinity Street, and on the left is Gledholt Methodist Church. 26 August 1964. (David Clarke)

Trinity Street descends towards the town centre near to Greenhead Park, whose eastern entrance is in the right background of this view. The cherry blossom is on the trees in this pleasant view of no. 586 climbing out of the town centre. This vehicle had re-entered service just a few weeks earlier bearing the body from no. 556. 19 May 1963. (Alan Dixon/Paul Watson)

Insides

A view of the upper deck of one of the 'three window' Park Royal bodied trolleys, in this case no. 549. Note the 'No Spitting' sign. 28 August 1963. (Tony Belton)

This is the lower deck of Roe-bodied no. 602, as passengers wait for its departure from Brackenhall terminus. Note the wooden panel on the front bulkhead, showing the fleet number in gold on the right, and the 'Roe' emblem on the left. (Fred Ivey)

Near the End

As well as the final year of the trolleybus, 1968 was also the centenary year of the founding of Huddersfield as a County Borough. The latter event was celebrated by a procession of floats through the town centre, telling the story of the town during this period. Each 20-year section of the parade was led by a suitable public transport exhibit, and for the period 1928 to 1948 a trolleybus was chosen. Accordingly, no. 631, spruced up and fitted with new trolley heads, was towed in the procession by derrick no. A9. It is seen here amidst the crowds of spectators at the John William Street/Westgate junction. 22 June 1968. (Mike Russell)

This glimpse inside Longroyd Bridge depot shortly before the end of trolleybus operations shows two of the remaining trolleybus fleet. In the background is one of the newly delivered Daimler Fleetline motorbuses ready to enter service and replace the last of the trolleys. (Malcolm King collection).

The highlight of the last week was the operation of an illuminated trolleybus. This was no. 623, which was dressed overall in coloured lights and bore 'Last Trolleybus' lettering. It entered public service in the early afternoon of Monday 8 July. It is seen here the previous day in Longroyd Bridge depot in all its glory, including white painted trolley poles.
7 July 1968. (Author)

At night, no. 623 looked quite a spectacle as demonstrated by this view of it at Lindley terminus. 12 July 1968. (Mike Russell)

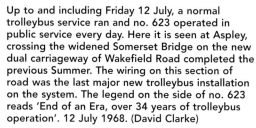

Up to and including Friday 12 July, a normal trolleybus service ran and no. 623 operated in public service every day. Here it is seen at Aspley, crossing the widened Somerset Bridge on the new dual carriageway of Wakefield Road completed the previous Summer. The wiring on this section of road was the last major new trolleybus installation on the system. The legend on the side of no. 623 reads 'End of an Era, over 34 years of trolleybus operation'. 12 July 1968. (David Clarke)

Looking down Westgate from Railway Street towards Kirkgate, it is 4.30pm on Friday 12 July, the last day of normal operations, and such a sight would not be seen again. On the left is no. 624 behind no. 632, both working to Waterloo, and on the right is no. 640 on a tea-time special journey to Salendine Nook. Only the latter vehicle would run after this day. 12 July 1968. (David Clarke)

The Last Day

The first notable event on the last day was the operation of a tour by preserved trolley no. 541, returning to the town for the first time since 1964. This vehicle had been donated by the Corporation to the National Trolleybus Association (NTA) and it was allowed to operate a morning tour for its members. Here it is seen turning from St George's Square into John William Street at 8.25am. The illuminated sign visible on the Transport Department Offices which read 'Huddersfield Public Transport Established 1882' had been erected there as part of the Borough Centenary celebrations. 13 July 1968. (David Clarke)

Only two trolleybuses were turned out on the morning of the last day, the remainder of the service being provided by motorbuses. No. 629 operated on route 73, and would become the last public service trolleybus that afternoon. Accordingly, as the morning wore on, it became fuller and fuller, and by mid-day was carrying a full standing load of passengers, all intent on being on board for the last ever journey. Already carrying a good load, it is seen turning at Outlane during the morning. 13 July 1968. (Robin Symons)

The other trolley in service was no. 640, which was operating route 71. In Wakefield Road, en route for Waterloo, it has encountered this pony and rider as they pass Ravensknowle Park. 13 July 1968. (Roland Box)

During the morning no. 638 was parked in St George's Square, where it is seen showing the destination setting which was displayed on the last trolleybus service journey on the previous evening (see page 72). When no. 640 broke down in Westgate just after mid-day, this vehicle took over its schedule, and later, at 3pm, it was used as one of the extra trolleybuses on the final run to Outlane. (Travel Lens Photographic)

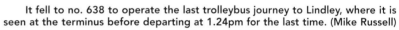

It fell to no. 638 to operate the last trolleybus journey to Lindley, where it is seen at the terminus before departing at 1.24pm for the last time. (Mike Russell)

Crowds, including many local residents, were out at Waterloo to see the last trolleys depart.
No. 627, now with 'The End' stickers on the front dash panel is the object of attention, but
there will be two more to come – no. 629 and last of all no. 623. 13 July 1968. (Mike Russell)

By the time the last trolleys had passed through the town centre towards Outlane, some sort of procession
had begun to form as is evident in this view of three trolleys passing the Salendine Nook Schools turning
loop. No. 638 is leading with no. 627 and no. 629 in the rear. No. 626 ran far ahead of the others, and had
departed from Outlane well before this trio reached the terminus. 13 July 1968. (Peter Lockwood)

The last public service trolleybus in Huddersfield poses with its crew at Outlane. The driver was Robert Collinson and his conductress was Florence Whittaker. Note the scribblings in the dust along the side of the vehicle. In the background no. 638 is departing for town. 13 July 1968. (Mike Russell)

No. 623 is seen arriving at Outlane followed by a motorcade in this view taken from the top deck of no. 627. No. 623's driver was C.P. Jones and Mona Lockwood was the conductress. Riding in the cab was the Transport Department's Overhead Line Superintendent. The motorbus on the left is the preserved Huddersfield wartime Daimler. 13 July 1968. (Roland Box)

The last one home. On arrival in the town centre, no. 629 turned from Westgate into Railway Street. Its crew took over the motorbus continuing 629's schedule, and a spare crew took over for the final trip through the Saturday afternoon shoppers to Longroyd Bridge depot. By the time no. 629 had arrived there, no. 623 was travelling along New Street to Buxton Road to allow its VIP passengers to alight near the Town Hall. From there it was towed away to Great Northern Street Works. This is the scene at Longroyd Bridge as no. 629 turns off Manchester Road into the forecourt of the depot, where again large crowds witnessed its arrival. 13 July 1968. (Alan Dixon /Paul Watson)

184

"On the return journey, the route was again lined with residents out to catch a last glimpse of the trolleybus; some waved handkerchiefs and others even waved flags! It seemed that the residents of Huddersfield turned out in greater numbers than those of any other town to abandon trolleybus operation in the 1960s. This was perhaps a tribute to the vehicles, perhaps a tribute to the publicity value of the excellent decorated trolleybus (one of the best ever) or simply a tribute to the local people."

Philip Jenkinson described his experience travelling on no. 629 on its last journey from Outlane

THE CONDUCTOR'S TALE

A few weeks in the life of a Huddersfield Trolleybus Conductor

by David Beach

In 1966/7/8 I was one of the student conductors employed by HCPTD during the summer holiday. One agreed to work for ten weeks, to justify the training, though in two subsequent summers I was allowed to 'sign on' for only eight weeks. By then, I think I was the only student conductor on the books, and for all I know I *may* have been the last of that particular genre.

I spent two days in the Conductor School at Great Northern Street Depot being trained by an avuncular inspector. They avoided the expense of equipping me with a PSV badge and thus had to restrict me to conducting trolleybuses, which being legally the same as trams were not covered by the PSV regulations. That suited me! For the 1968 season, they needed to get me a PSV.

Training consisted mainly of mastering the Ultimate ticket machine, different types of passes, rules and regulations, and money handling. At Longroyd Bridge I was instructed in raising and lowering the booms, and shown the mess and cashing-up rooms. In the town centre the Union Shop Steward was there to receive 'subs', and I was clearly expected to be a member of the T&GWU during that time. After two days I was put in the experienced hands of Florence Whittaker, to try things out for real. She put me upstairs on the Bradley-bound trolley, cigarette smoking workers on the way to ICI for a morning shift. Fortunately they all handed the correct money and there were no complications. The next day she put me on downstairs only, so there was a bell to ring and a platform to supervise. At some point she must have put me on to frog-pulling too. On the third day I ran the whole show while she just hung around to keep an eye on me. She was a very good teacher to have.

Most staff were on a rota with a regular mate, and would know their duties for weeks ahead, but staff who were new, or who had not formed a partnership with a particular driver, or had asked for overtime, would look up their duties for that week on the "Change sheet". Even those on rotas had a few days each month when they would be on the Change Sheet, maybe to help keep up their route knowledge.

Main duties would be early turn, late turn, or 'spreadover'. Blocks of duty tended to come as three early turns followed by three late turns, maybe with a spreadover in the middle, followed by one or two days off. One never had to finish at midnight one day and start at 05.00 the next. The department were good about arranging days off if specifically requested, so I was not at work on the day of the trolleybus closure, for example.

An early turn required arrival at Longroyd Bridge sometime after 5am, with a finish round about 1pm. A late turn started around 3pm, picking up the bus in the town centre, and finishing at the depot close to midnight. The gap between the two duties would be covered by overtime and by staff on spreadover duties. These ran from around 07.00 until 10.00, and then 13.00 to 19.00 approx, thereby covering two rush-hours and the interregnum at lunchtime. Spreadover duties knocked-out a whole day, but you did get paid something for the time you were not actually conducting, and you had more civilised times for getting up and going to bed. I quite liked them.

For staff making an early start or late finish, there were staff buses, using the o.m.o. single deckers, which toured the more populous suburbs. I used the night bus to get home a few times, being tired after a long shift, but in the morning always walked to Longroyd Bridge. Walking

The conductor pulls the trigger on Leeds Road, allowing no. 631 to turn into Brooklands on its way to Keldregate. (Travel Lens Photographic)

through an almost deserted town centre at 05.00 was a slightly creepy experience and one I recall with pleasure. For a slightly later start one could always catch a service bus. You picked up the ticket machine in its metal box, complete with spare tickets, and already had a cash bag and the ten shilling 'float' – perfectly adequate when the average fare was 4d and most passengers paid in coppers. A board on the wall just inside the depot showed the 'schedule' number, and alongside it the number of the trolleybus to be used and the number of the lane in which it could be found. The night shift had to plan as the trolleybuses returned to depot the night before, making sure that any on 'light duties' were allocated to just the morning rush hour, for example. On the Change Sheet one could get a different driver every day, usually the ones who had no permanent crew partner. One prepared one's waybill, set the blinds, and set off straight into town.

Crews on Early Turns could get some breakfast. Somewhere on the route you could buy a sandwich and a can of tea. At Meg Lane on the Longwood route a shopkeeper did this – you would place an order on the previous trip. At Outlane the sweetshop in the stone cabin at the terminus provided a similar service. At Lindley a housewife made excellent fried-egg sandwiches.

The breakfast 'break' was achieved by a scheduling procedure known as 'dropping back'. A trolleybus scheduled to be running all day would have twenty minutes or so of extra lay-over while the next timetabled journey would be covered by the following trolleybus and crew, probably on a spreadover or morning overtime, prior to returning to depot. So it was necessary to lower the booms to let them through. On the surviving trolleybus routes in that summer, these extended layovers happened at Outlane, Lindley, or Longwood.

On an early shift, knocking off occurred in the town centre, and the conductor had to pay in at the main offices. The value of tickets had to be calculated and covered by the money handed in. If you lost money it came out of wages. A sizeable number of bags of coins needed to be dealt with, and one's hands became quite filthy from the coppers. At rush hour, with no time to bag up pennies, the cash bag became like a millstone. Some conductors solved this by giving lots of pennies in change, rather than three-penny bits and sixpences. This was understandable but also rather irritated the passengers. After ten weeks of conducting, and it was quite a hot summer, I had lost two stone of weight.

One of the jobs on the 'Change Sheet' was to be a 'Spare', to cover a conductor failing to turn up for his duty.

The 'dropping-back' procedure, allowing crews an extended break at the terminus, is demonstrated here. At Newsome South, the crew of no. 626 has lowered its trolley poles to allow no. 625, on the right to overtake once it has completed the reversing manoeuvre. (Tony Belton)

Just occasionally I was instructed [despite my lack of PSV badge] to conduct a motorbus, and found myself at Taylor Hill or Bailiff Bridge, having no route knowledge and depending on the passengers knowing the fare and where to get off. On one occasion a driver for a Beaumont Park [single deck o.m.o.] bus failed to show up, and had to be replaced by a spare driver who had no training on the ticket machines and no route knowledge. So I, who also had no route knowledge, was put with him as conductor. We had to ask passengers which way to go, and getting them to walk past the driver and give me the money instead became quite a challenge.

The fun of trolleybus conducting was, of course, when things went wrong. Dewirements were quite rare but entertaining when they happened. On one journey from Bradley we were forced to slow down at the Keldregate junction, and again at the Deighton reverser, to allow negotiation of the overhead junctions. This so irritated the driver of a refuse truck that he was subsequently fined and banned for what the Examiner described as a "Near-attack on a bus'. I was the chief witness for the prosecution.

I had a few disagreements with passengers, notably with a slightly tipsy 'mutton-dressed-as-lamb' passenger who had been out on the town, and who missed her stop at Greenside [Waterloo] because 'I had not rung the bell'. The fact she was upstairs and therefore out of sight, likewise the written instruction on the bell strip to 'Press once to stop', cut no ice with that particularly disagreeable individual.

On one occasion a passenger boarding a Longwood trolley contrived to spill an entire 4-pint tin of grey gloss paint all over the saloon floor alongside the long seats, leaving just a narrow causeway of dry floor. I turned the seat squabs upside down, and gave verbal warnings, but still one elderly gentleman walked right into the paint and sat on the upturned seat-squab and then looked puzzled. Naturally we had a change-over vehicle once we got back to Longroyd Bridge. I quite enjoyed, too, the occasion on the first bus of the morning to Waterloo when the first passenger from there was a school friend who clearly had not spent the night in his own bed, and was somewhat embarrassed to be caught out!

And so to the end of the day. One dreaded the late night buses on a Friday and Saturday night in case there were belligerent drunks on board. I was lucky and had no trouble, though a crew on a Brackenhall bus were so badly beaten up that the staff withdrew late night buses for several weeks in protest. If the last outbound journey could be fraught with anxiety, the return to depot could be positively exhilarating. With hardly any passengers, and timing points being honoured in the breach, it could be quite a fast journey on almost deserted roads. It was an opportunity to work out the value of tickets in the hope that no-one else would get on, though I did run the risk of getting into trouble for issuing four 'penny' tickets for a 4d fare as I had already calculated all the other ticket numbers. On a different occasion, returning from Bradley, I stood at the front of the lower saloon of a speeding homebound trolleybus, with the window through to the cab open, leaning over the control box and watching the road ahead, and the lights shining on the wires. Magical.

And then cashing up, and a walk home or a lift on the crew bus.

In all I did 26 weeks of conducting spread over three summers, though the last of these was almost exclusively on diesels following the closure of the trolleybus system. It was hard work but great fun, and lots of wonderful memories.

AFTERLIFE

A total of 21 Huddersfield trolleybuses had a significant life after being withdrawn from service in their home town. Their story is told here.

The Reading Connection

Nos 7 to 18, withdrawn in 1948, were sold for £200 each to Reading Corporation Transport Department, desperate to acquire additional vehicles to cater for the post-war boom in passenger numbers. On delivery to Reading, it was found that their condition was much worse than had been thought, and their entry into service was a slow process. In fact, only six of the vehicles were put on the road, the remainder being stored for spare parts before being scrapped.

Those which operated in Reading were:
No. 414 (Reading no. 158) in service from September 1948
No. 410 (Reading no. 159) in service from April 1949
No. 408 (Reading no. 160) in service from February 1949
No. 412 (Reading no. 162) in service from December 1949
No. 416 (Reading no. 161) in service from February 1951
No. 409 (Reading no. 163) in service from June 1950
All six ran until 1955/56, nos 161, 162 and 163 surviving until the end of the latter year.

The first Huddersfield trolleybus to enter service in Reading was no. 158, which is seen here at Tilehurst terminus on 6 March 1949, the same day that the Brackenhall and Riddings routes opened it its home town. Note that the dummy radiator outline below the cab has been removed, as has the route number display. (W.J. Haynes / British Trolleybus Society collection)

Reading no. 162 (Huddersfield no 412) stands at Kentwood terminus in March 1952. This was the vehicle that overturned at Outlane in 1938. (W.J. Haynes / British Trolleybus Society collection)

This is Huddersfield no. 12 (later 412) on its side at Leeches Hill, Outlane in October 1938.
(J.P. Senior collection)

Reading no. 158 is at Whitley Wood terminus in the early 1950s. Note the change of livery style on the front dash panel to that shown in the earlier photo of this vehicle.
(Author's collection)

The six vehicles not placed in service at Reading were stored in the open on land which was eventually used for a new depot. From left to right in this view dated 23 December 1950 are nos. 417, 411 and 413. All were scrapped in 1952. Note they all bear the original Huddersfield trolleybus livery.
(J.H. Meredith)

The final withdrawal of the ex-Huddersfield vehicles in Reading was not the end of the town's connection with Huddersfield's trolleys. Almost twelve years later, another such vehicle appeared – this being the newly preserved Huddersfield no. 631, which ran a tour of the Berkshire town for trolleybus fans on Sunday 27 October 1968, shortly before the Reading system closed. It left Huddersfield on tow in the early evening of the previous day and travelled overnight via the M1 motorway to London, the North Circular Road and then the A4 to Reading, arriving at their depot at 7.30am. After checks and testing, it performed faultlessly on the tour before being parked at the premises of a local coach company (Smith's Luxury Coaches) pending further operation elsewhere (see pages 195-196).

Seen at Reading's Mill Lane depot, no. 631 is alongside the ex-Belfast trolleybus that also operated on that day. In the background, between the two vehicles, can be seen the Scammell towing vehicle that brought no. 631 from Yorkshire. (Robert Mack)

No. 631 turns at the Wokingham Road terminus during the tour. (Author)

A Matter of Convenience

In 1954, six withdrawn Karriers were sold, without trolley gear and electrical equipment, to Epsom and Ewell Council in Surrey. Five of these were converted into mobile public toilets for use on Epsom Downs race course (where the Derby is held). The sixth was used as a store room. The vehicles concerned were:

No. 488	Epsom no. 1 (Ladies)
No. 452	Epsom no, 2 (Gentlemen)
No. 489	Epsom no. 3 (Ladies)
No. 470	Epsom no. 4 (Gentlemen)
No. 459	Epsom no. 5 (Ladies)
No. 471	Store room

Painted cream with green bands, including the swoop at the front, they were a familiar sight at race meetings for sixteen years until their last outing in April 1970. Thus they had served race-goers for just as long as they had run in their home town. When taken out of use, all five toilet units were purchased by transport societies. Nos 1 and 2 went to the Sittingbourne and Kemsley narrow gauge railway in Kent: nos 3 and 5 went to the National Trolleybus Association. No. 4 was purchased by the West Riding Trolleybus Society, being taken to Sandtoft on 25 May 1970, and later to the 'Arch' storage unit in Huddersfield pending restoration to Huddersfield condition. Unfortunately its very poor condition prevented this and following the collapse of the bodywork, the chassis was taken to Sandtoft where it was cosmetically restored and is now on display. The other examples did not fare any better and none of these now exist.

Epsom no. 4 is seen in situ at Epsom Downs racecourse. Apart from the livery, there were minimal changes to the external appearance of these units. In its later years at Epsom, no. 3 suffered accident damage to its front end and was given new cab windows and very flat dash panelling. (Tony Belton)

The only vehicle purchased by Epsom and Ewell Council not converted into a toilet was no. 471, which was used as a store. It is seen here in the early 1950s at St George's Square. In the background is no 526, passing a rebuilt pre-war Karrier. (Jim Copland/Paul Watson)

Epsom and Ewell toilets nos 1 and 2 are seen here after transfer to the Sittingbourne and Kemsley Light Railway. Here, they were hurriedly repainted into the livery of the Locomotive Club of Great Britain who ran the operation. Former Huddersfield no. 488 is on the left, with no. 452 on the right. (Malcolm King collection)

The only remaining relic of the Epsom toilets is the chassis of no. 470, seen here after the remains of its body had been removed (see page 229). It was subsequently cosmetically restored and placed on display at Sandtoft. (Bruce Lake)

A Trio Preserved

Three complete trolleys have survived in operating condition and all are resident at The Trolleybus Museum at Sandtoft near Doncaster.

Preserved vehicles lined up at The Trolleybus Museum Sandtoft. From the left is derrick A9 (owned by the Keighley Bus Museum), no. 619, no. 631 and no. 541. (Paul Watson)

No. 541

Withdrawn after operating the last trolleybus journey to Crosland Hill on 5 February 1964, this vehicle, the first post-war member of the fleet, was presented to the National Trolleybus Association. After being formally handed over to them on 21 June 1964, it was moved to an open site at Plumtree Station in Nottinghamshire. On 22 May 1966 it ran a tour over the Wolverhampton system, thus making history by becoming the first preserved trolleybus outside London to operate under its own power, and the first ever to run under 'foreign' wires.

No. 541 is seen at Plumtree Station in company with Manchester Crossley six-wheeler no. 1250 and Nottingham wartime austerity Karrier 4-wheeler no. 466. Both the latter vehicles survive, no. 1250 at the Greater Manchester Museum of Transport, and no. 466 at Sandtoft. (Tony Belton)

The Fighting Cocks terminus at Wolverhampton plays host to no. 541 on 22 May 1966. (Fred Ivey)

After running at Huddersfield on the last day, it was stored at various locations, including Sandtoft, Four Marks in Hampshire and North Woolwich in London. It returned to Sandtoft on 9 October 1985, eventually undergoing extensive restoration. The fully restored vehicle was launched into service at Sandtoft on 29 August 2010. In 2013 it visited the East Anglia Transport Museum and ran on their wiring circuit, the first time this century that one of the preserved Huddersfield trio has operated away from Sandtoft.

Both trams and trolleybuses run side by side at the East Anglia Transport Museum at Carlton Colville. Here, no. 541 meets trams from Blackpool and London on 14 September 2013. (John Parkin)

No. 619

This vehicle was purchased after the closure of the system by the BUT Preservation Group, which included David Haigh, Bill Roberts, and Philip Singleton. It had been taken out of service on after 30 May 1968, purely because its Road Fund licence expired at the end of that month. Initially, it was stored locally in a field at Meltham, but left there on 4 January 1969 when it was towed north to Middlesbrough to operate a tour of the Tees-side trolleybus routes on the 12

of that month. After this event, it spent short periods in store at Rastrick then Baildon, before going to Sandtoft in October 1969. On 12 September 1972 it made history by becoming the first trolleybus to operate under its own power on the site, albeit using battery power. Its later history included being located at the West Yorkshire Transport Museum at Ludlam Street, Bradford, and then at the short-lived Transperience museum site at Low Moor.

It was a damp and dreary day when no. 619 toured the Tees-side system. The operation of a long six-wheel trolleybus presented several problems on the day, and this scene shows the aftermath of a dewirement that required some repairs to the vehicle's trolley booms as well as to the overhead wiring. In typical Tees-side scenery, no. 619 is being passed by one of the 'home' fleet. On the right is the former Bradford Leyland motorbus which towed no. 619 north, and is itself today under restoration at Sandtoft. (Author)

A tight fit for no. 619 as it crawls under the very low Subway bridge at Grangetown. (David Beach)

Following the demise of the Transperience project, the vehicle passed to another group consisting of Bruce Lake, Steve Harrison, and both versions of the Jenkinson brothers, Philip and Keith, under whose ownership it returned to Sandtoft on 1 August 1998. Following an external repaint, it returned to Huddersfield in August 2001 being displayed in St George's Square and attending the Historic Commercial Vehicle rally at Greenhead Park. It has since been a stalwart member of Sandtoft's operational fleet year-in year-out.

On returning to Sandtoft, the new owners of no. 619 restored the vehicle to its former glory. It is seen during this process in a largely anonymous state. (Author's collection)

No. 631

Representative of the newest six-wheeled trolleybuses to be used in Britain, no. 631 was purchased by the Huddersfield Trolleybus Preservation Society, formed by three teenagers: David Beach, Bas Longbottom and the author. The vehicle was chosen because it was generally regarded, both by the Transport Department and enthusiasts, to be in very good condition. It last operated on 11 July 1968, two days before the closure, when it ran on the Outlane route. It was purchased for £100, this matching the highest bid tendered by the scrap dealers. Collected from Longroyd Bridge depot in mid-August, it was transferred to secure storage at the 'Arch', a space underneath Hudderfield's railway viaduct which had been recently rented by local bus preservationists, and situated very close to the Great Northern Street Works of the Transport Department. However, it did not languish there, and in October it was towed south to

Reading as already described, and then to Bournemouth, where it toured the trolleybus system on 24 November 1968. During this event it was turned on the turntable at Christchurch terminus, and it therefore became the only trolleybus to have stood on both publicly accessible turntables in Britain. After these wanderings, no. 631 returned to the Arch, remaining until October 1969 when it was transferred to the newly established Sandtoft museum site. 1983 was the centenary of public transport operation in Huddersfield, and accordingly no. 631 returned to its home town to be displayed over the pits at the Great Northern Street Works at the open days commemorating the event. It was also displayed at the bus station and took part in the Mayor's Parade. Prior to these events the West Yorkshire Passenger Transport Executive (the public body then running passenger transport in the town) arranged for the vehicle to receive a full repaint.

No. 631 is manoeuvred into its new home at the Arch in August 1968, having been towed from Longroyd Bridge depot by former County Motors Guy Arab motorbus no. 70, also an Arch resident. (Author)

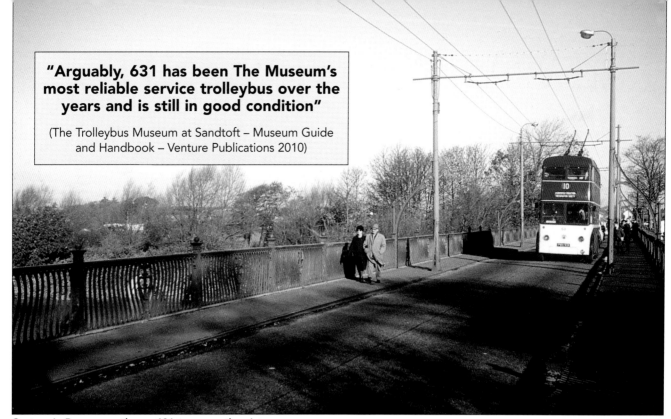

"Arguably, 631 has been The Museum's most reliable service trolleybus over the years and is still in good condition"

(The Trolleybus Museum at Sandtoft – Museum Guide and Handbook – Venture Publications 2010)

On tour in Bournemouth, no. 631 traverses the picturesque Tuckton Bridge near Christchurch. (Author's collection)

Since then and up to very recently, the vehicle has remained at Sandtoft as one of the operational fleet, being in use every year, and its ownership is now with the British Trolleybus Society. In 2012 it was decorated to celebrate the Queen's Diamond Jubilee, these embellishments being by intention very much in the style of those carried by no. 535 in 1953 to celebrate the Coronation. After the 2012 museum season, it was withdrawn from service and sent to Swindon to the premises of Thamesdown Transport for full refurbishment and repainting. The vehicle returned to Sandtoft after repainting and internal refurbishment in May 2014, and was re-launched into service at the end of July.

In action at Sandtoft in October 2012, no. 631 carries decorations celebrating the Queen's Diamond Jubilee. (Author)

PRE-WAR TROLLEYBUS FLEET

(Until 1942, vehicles were numbered No.1 to No.140)

Fleet no.	Reg no.	Chassis type	Motor HP	Body	SC	Into service	Out of service	Note
401	VH 5723	RSJ D6	RSJ 80	Brush	60	1933	1946	
402	VH 5724	K E6	BTH 80	Park Royal	60	1933	1947	
403	VH 5725	K E6	BTH 80	Park Royal	60	1933	1947	
404	VH 5726	S MS2	BTH 80	Park Royal	60	1933	1943	
405	VH 5727	K E6	EE 80	E.Electric	60	1933	1947	
406	VH 5728	AEC 663T	EE 80	E.Electric	60	1933	1946	
407	VH 6750	K E6	MV 80	Brush	64	1934	1948	B
408	VH 6751	K E6	MV 80	Brush	64	1934	1948	B
409	VH 6752	K E6	MV 80	Brush	64	1934	1948	B
410	VH 6753	K E6	MV 80	Brush	64	1934	1948	B
411	VH 6754	K E6	MV 80	Brush	64	1934	1948	B
412	VH 6755	K E6	MV 80	Brush	64	1934	1948	B
413	VH 6756	K E6	MV 80	Brush	64	1934	1948	B
414	VH 6757	K E6	MV 80	Brush	64	1934	1948	B
415	VH 6758	K E6	MV 80	Brush	64	1934	1948	B
416	VH 6759	K E6	MV 80	Brush	64	1934	1948	B
417	VH 6760	K E6	MV 80	Brush	64	1934	1948	B
418	VH 6761	K E6	MV 80	Brush	64	1934	1948	B
419	VH 6765	K E6	MV 80	Park Royal	64	1934	1948	
420	VH 6767	K E6	MV 80	Park Royal	64	1934	1948	
421	VH 6766	K E6	MV 80	Park Royal	64	1934	1948	
422	VH 6768	K E6	MV 80	Park Royal	64	1934	1948	
423	VH 6771	K E6	EE 80	Park Royal	64	1934	1948	
424	VH 6772	K E6	EE 80	Park Royal	64	1934	1948	
425	VH 6769	K E6	MV 80	Park Royal	64	1934	1948	
426	VH 6762	K E6	MV 80	Park Royal	64	1934	1948	
427	VH 6770	K E6	MV 80	Park Royal	64	1934	1948	
428	VH 6773	K E6	EE 80	Park Royal	64	1934	1948	R(PR) 41
429	VH 6763	K E6	MV 80	Park Royal	64	1934	1948	
430	VH 6764	K E6	MV 80	Park Royal	64	1934	1948	
431	VH 8722	K E6	MV 95	Weymann	64	1936	1949	
432	VH 8530	K E6	MV 95	Park Royal	64	1935	1949	
433	VH 9933	K E6	MV 95	Park Royal	64	1937	1949	
434	VH 9934	K E6	MV 95	Park Royal	64	1937	1949	
435	VH 9935	K E6	MV 95	Park Royal	64	1937	1949	
436	VH 9936	K E6	MV 95	Park Royal	64	1937	1949	
437	VH 9937	K E6	MV 95	Park Royal	64	1937	1949	
438	VH 9938	K E6	MV 95	Park Royal	64	1937	1948	A
439	VH 9939	K E6	MV 95	Park Royal	64	1937	1949	
440	VH 9940	K E6	MV 95	Park Royal	64	1937	1949	
441	AVH 441	K E6	MV 95	Park Royal	64	1937	1949	
442	AVH 442	S E6	MV 95	Park Royal	64	1937	1949	
443	AVH 443	K E6	MV 95	Park Royal	64	1937	1949	
444	AVH 444	AEC E6	MV 95	Park Royal	64	1937	1951	
445	AVH 445	K E6	MV 95	Park Royal	64	1937	1949	
446	AVH 446	K E6	MV 95	Park Royal	64	1937	1950	
447	AVH 447	K E6	MV 95	Park Royal	64	1937	1949	
448	AVH 448	K E6	MV 95	Park Royal	64	1937	1951	
449	AVH 449	K E6	MV 95	Park Royal	64	1937	1951	
450	AVH 450	K E6	MV 95	Park Royal	64	1937	1951	
451	AVH 451	K E6	MV 95	Park Royal	64	1937	1951	

Fleet no.	Reg no.	Chassis type	Motor HP	Body	SC	Into service	Out of service	Note
452	AVH 452	K E6	MV 95	Park Royal	64	1937	1953	C
453	AVH 453	K E6	MV 95	Park Royal	64	1937	1951	
454	AVH 454	K E6	MV 95	Park Royal	64	1937	1951	
455	AVH 455	K E6	MV 95	Park Royal	64	1937	1951	
456	AVH 456	K E6	MV 95	Park Royal	64	1937	1951	
457	AVH 457	K E6	MV 95	Park Royal	64	1937	1950	
458	AVH 458	K E6	MV 95	Park Royal	64	1937	1950	
459	AVH 459	K E6	MV 95	Park Royal	64	1937	1953	C
460	AVH 460	K E6	MV 95	Park Royal	64	1937	1952	
461	AVH 461	K E6	MV 95	Park Royal	64	1938	1951	
462	AVH 462	K E6	MV 95	Park Royal	64	1938	1953	
463	AVH 463	K E6	MV 95	Park Royal	64	1938	1951	
464	AVH 464	K E6	MV 95	Park Royal	64	1938	1953	
465	AVH 465	K E6	MV 95	Park Royal	64	1938	1950	
466	AVH 466	K E6	MV 95	Park Royal	64	1938	1952	
467	AVH 467	K E6	MV 95	Park Royal	64	1938	1953	
468	AVH 468	K E6	MV 95	Park Royal	64	1938	1951	
469	AVH 469	K E6	MV 95	Park Royal	64	1938	1951	
470	AVH 470	K E6	MV 95	Park Royal	64	1938	1953	C, Pc
471	AVH 471	K E6	MV 95	Park Royal	64	1938	1953	C
472	AVH 472	K E6	MV 95	Park Royal	64	1938	1951	
473	AVH 473	K E6	MV 95	Park Royal	64	1938	1953	
474	AVH 474	K E6	MV 95	Park Royal	64	1938	1953	
475	AVH 475	K E6	MV 95	Park Royal	64	1938	1959	R(Ro) 52
476	AVH 476	K E6	MV 95	Park Royal	64	1938	1959	
477	AVH 477	K E6	MV 95	Park Royal	64	1938	1955	
478	AVH 478	K E6	MV 95	Park Royal	64	1938	1956	
479	AVH 479	K E6	MV 95	Park Royal	64	1938	1956	
480	AVH 480	K E6	MV 95	Park Royal	64	1938	1950	
481	AVH 481	K E6	MV 95	Park Royal	64	1938	1955	
482	AVH 482	K E6	MV 95	Park Royal	64	1938	1956	
483	AVH 483	K E6	MV 95	Park Royal	64	1938	1956	
484	AVH 484	K E6	MV 95	Park Royal	64	1938	1959	R (Ro) 53
485	AVH 485	K E6	MV 95	Park Royal	64	1938	1955	
486	AVH 486	K E6	MV 95	Park Royal	64	1938	1955	
487	AVH 487	K E6	MV 95	Park Royal	64	1938	1955	
488	AVH 488	K E6	MV 95	Park Royal	64	1938	1953	C
489	AVH 489	K E6	MV 95	Park Royal	64	1938	1953	C
490	AVH 490	K E6	MV 95	Park Royal	64	1938	1955	
491	AVH 491	K E6	MV 95	Park Royal	64	1938	1959	R(Ro) 51
492	AVH 492	K E6	MV 95	Park Royal	64	1938	1962	R(Ro) 51
493	AVH 493	K E6	MV 95	Park Royal	64	1938	1962	R(Ro) 50
494	AVH 494	K E6	MV 95	Park Royal	64	1938	1962	R(Ro) 50
495	AVH 495	K E6	MV 95	Park Royal	64	1938	1955	
496	AVH 496	K E6	MV 95	Park Royal	64	1938	1959	R(Ro) 51
497	AVH 497	K E6	MV 95	Park Royal	64	1938	1962	R(Ro) 50
498	AVH 498	K E6	MV 95	Park Royal	64	1938	1959	R(Ro) 51
499	AVH 499	K E6	MV 95	Park Royal	64	1939	1959	R(Ro) 51
500	AVH 500	K E6	MV 95	Park Royal	64	1939	1956	
501	AVH 501	K E6	MV 95	Park Royal	64	1939	1962	R(Ro) 51
502	AVH 502	K E6	MV 95	Park Royal	64	1939	1959	R(Ro) 51
503	AVH 503	K E6	MV 95	Park Royal	64	1939	1962	R(Ro) 51
504	AVH 504	K E6	MV 95	Park Royal	64	1939	1945	A
505	AVH 505	K E6	MV 95	Park Royal	64	1939	1956	
506	AVH 506	K E6	MV 95	Brush	64	1939	1949	
507	AVH 507	K E6	MV 95	Brush	64	1938	1949	
508	AVH 508	K E6	MV 95	Brush	64	1938	1962	R(Ro) 51
509	AVH 509	K E6	MV 95	Brush	64	1938	1959	R(Ro) 51
510	AVH 510	K E6	MV 95	Brush	64	1938	1949	
511	AVH 511	K E6	MV 95	Brush	64	1938	1949	
512	AVH 512	K E6	MV 95	Brush	64	1938	1949	
513	AVH 513	K E6	MV 95	Brush	64	1938	1949	

Fleet no.	Reg no.	Chassis type	Motor HP	Body	SC	Into service	Out of service	Note
514	AVH 514	K E6	MV 95	Brush	64	1938	1949	
515	AVH 515	K E6	MV 95	Brush	64	1939	1947	
516	AVH 516	K E6	EE 100	Weymann	64	1940	1955	
517	AVH 517	K E6	EE 100	Weymann	64	1940	1961	R(Ro) 53
518	AVH 518	K E6	EE 100	Weymann	64	1940	1961	R(Ro) 53
519	AVH 519	K E6	EE 100	Weymann	64	1940	1962	R(Ro) 53
520	AVH 520	K E6	EE 100	Weymann	64	1940	1955	
521	AVH 521	K E6	EE 100	Weymann	64	1940	1955	
522	AVH 522	K E6	EE 100	Weymann	64	1940	1955	
523	AVH 523	K E6	EE 100	Weymann	64	1940	1963	R(Ro) 53
524	AVH 524	K E6	EE 100	Weymann	64	1940	1961	R(Ro) 54
525	AVH 525	K E6	EE 100	Weymann	64	1940	1963	R(Ro) 52
526	BVH 126	K E6	MV 95	Park Royal	64	1939	1956	
527	BVH 127	K E6	MV 95	Park Royal	64	1939	1963	R(Ro) 54
528	BVH 128	K E6	MV 95	Park Royal	64	1939	1963	R(Ro) 53
529	BVH 129	K E6	MV 95	Park Royal	64	1939	1963	R(Ro) 53
530	BVH 130	K E6	MV 95	Park Royal	64	1939	1955	
531	BVH 131	K E6	MV 95	Park Royal	64	1939	1959	
532	BVH 132	K E6	MV 95	Park Royal	64	1939	1963	R(Ro) 53
533	BVH 133	K E6	MV 95	Park Royal	64	1939	1956	
534	BVH 134	K E6	MV 95	Park Royal	64	1939	1956	
535	BVH 135	K E6	MV 95	Park Royal	64	1939	1963	R(Ro) 53
536	BVH 136	K E6	MV 95	Park Royal	64	1939	1963	R(Ro) 53
537	BVH 137	K E6	MV 95	Park Royal	64	1939	1956	
538	BVH 138	K E6	MV 95	Park Royal	64	1939	1955	
539	BVH 139	K E6	MV 95	Park Royal	64	1939	1956	
540	BVH 140	K E6	MV 95	Park Royal	64	1939	1961	R(Ro) 53

No. 540 was the highest numbered pre-war trolleybus. It is seen here at the Bradley stop in John William Street in the early 1950s, shortly before its chassis was rebuilt and fitted with new Roe bodywork. (Roy Marshall)

POST-WAR TROLLEYBUS FLEET

Fleet no.	Reg no.	Chassis type	Motor HP	Body	SC	Into service	Out of service	Note
541	CVH 741	K MS2	MV 125	Park Royal	70	1947	1964	P
542	CVH 742	K MS2	MV 125	Park Royal	70	1947	1964	
543	CVH 743	K MS2	MV 125	Park Royal	70	1947	1967	R(EL) 61
544	CVH 744	K MS2	MV 125	Park Royal	70	1947	1964	
545	CVH 745	K MS2	MV 125	Park Royal	70	1947	1964	R(EL) 61 A
546	CVH 746	K MS2	MV 125	Park Royal	70	1947	1967	R(EL) 61
547	CVH 747	K MS2	MV 125	Park Royal	70	1947	1964	
548	CVH 748	K MS2	MV 125	Park Royal	70	1947	1967	R(EL) 61
549	DVH 49	K MS2	MV 125	Park Royal	70	1948	1965	
550	DVH 50	K MS2	MV 125	Park Royal	70	1948	1963	R(Ro) 58
551	DVH 51	K MS2	MV 125	Park Royal	70	1948	1963	R(EL) 55
552	DVH 52	K MS2	MV 125	Park Royal	70	1948	1963	R(EL) 55
553	DVH 53	K MS2	MV 125	Park Royal	70	1948	1965	R(EL) 55
554	DVH 54	K MS2	MV 125	Park Royal	70	1948	1965	R(EL) 55
555	DVH 55	K MS2	MV 125	Park Royal	70	1948	1965	R(EL) 55
556	DVH 56	K MS2	MV 125	Park Royal	70	1948	1962	R(EL) 55 E
557	DVH 57	K MS2	MV 125	Park Royal	70	1948	1962	R(EL) 55 E
558	DVH 58	K MS2	MV 125	Park Royal	70	1948	1963	R(EL) 55
559	DVH 59	K MS2	MV 125	Park Royal	70	1948	1963	R(EL) 56
560	DVH 60	K MS2	MV 125	Park Royal	70	1948	1964	R(EL) 56
561	DVH 61	K MS2	MV 125	Park Royal	70	1948	1963	R(EL) 56 E
562	DVH 62	K MS2	MV 125	Park Royal	70	1948	1964	R(EL) 56
563	DVH 63	K MS2	MV 125	Park Royal	70	1948	1963	R(EL) 56 E
564	DVH 64	K MS2	MV 125	Park Royal	70	1948	1964	R(EL) 57
565	DVH 65	K MS2	MV 125	Park Royal	70	1948	1964	R(EL) 57
566	DVH 66	K MS2	MV 125	Park Royal	70	1948	1963	R(EL) 57
567	DVH 67	K MS2	MV 125	Park Royal	70	1948	1963	R(Ro) 58
568	DVH 68	K MS2	MV 125	Park Royal	70	1948	1964	R(Ro) 58
569	ECX 169	S MS2	MV 125	Park Royal	70	1949	1964	R(Ro) 58
570	ECX 170	S MS2	MV 125	Park Royal	70	1949	1964	R(EL) 57
571	ECX 171	S MS2	MV 125	Park Royal	70	1949	1964	R(Ro) 58
572	ECX 172	S.MS2	MV 125	Park Royal	70	1949	1964	R(Ro) 59
573	ECX 173	S MS2	MV 125	Park Royal	70	1949	1965	R(EL) 57
574	ECX 174	S MS2	MV 125	Park Royal	70	1949	1965	R(Ro) 59
575	ECX 175	S MS2	MV 125	Park Royal	70	1949	1965	R(Ro) 59
576	ECX 176	S MS2	MV 125	Park Royal	70	1949	1965	R(Ro) 59
577	ECX 177	S MS2	MV 125	Park Royal	70	1949	1965	R(Ro) 59
578	ECX 178	S MS2	MV 125	Park Royal	70	1949	1965	R(Ro) 59
579	ECX 179	S MS2	MV 125	Park Royal	70	1949	1965	R(Ro) 59
580	ECX 180	S MS2	MV 125	Park Royal	70	1949	1965	R(Ro) 59
581	ECX 181	S MS2	MV 125	Park Royal	70	1949	1965	R(Ro) 59
582	ECX 182	S MS2	MV 125	Park Royal	70	1949	1967	R(EL) 62
583	ECX 183	S MS2	MV 125	Park Royal	70	1949	1967	R(EL) 62
584	ECX 184	S MS2	MV 125	Park Royal	70	1949	1967	R(EL) 62
585	ECX 185	S MS2	MV 125	Park Royal	70	1949	1967	R(EL) 62 A
586	ECX 186	S MS2	MV 125	Park Royal	70	1949	1965	R(EL) 63 E
587	ECX 187	S MS2	MV 125	Park Royal	70	1949	1965	R(EL) 63 E
588	ECX 188	S MS2	MV 125	Park Royal	70	1949	1965	
589	ECX 189	S MS2	MV 125	Park Royal	70	1949	1965	R(Ro) 59
590	ECX 190	S MS2	MV 125	Park Royal	70	1949	1965	
591	ECX 191	S MS2	MV 125	Park Royal	70	1949	1965	R(EL) 63 E
592	ECX 192	S MS2	MV 125	Park Royal	70	1949	1965	R(EL) 63 E
593	FCX 293	S MS2	MV 125	Roe	70	1950	1965	
594	FCX 294	S MS2	MV 125	Roe	70	1951	1964	

Fleet no.	Reg no.	Chassis type	Motor HP	Body	SC	Into service	Out of service	Note
595	FCX 295	S MS2	MV 125	Roe	70	1951	1966	
596	FCX 296	S MS2	MV 125	Roe	70	1951	1966	
597	FCX 297	S MS2	MV 125	Roe	70	1951	1966	
598	FCX 298	S MS2	MV 125	Roe	70	1951	1966	
599	FCX 299	S MS2	MV 125	Roe	70	1951	1965	
600	FCX 800	S MS2	MV 125	Roe	70	1951	1966	
601	FCX 801	S MS2	MV 125	Roe	70	1951	1966	
602	FCX 802	S MS2	MV 125	Roe	70	1951	1966	
603	FCX 803	S MS2	MV 125	Roe	70	1951	1966	
604	FCX 804	S MS2	MV 125	Roe	70	1951	1966	
605	FCX 805	S MS2	MV 125	Roe	70	1951	1966	D
606	FCX 806	S MS2	MV 125	Roe	70	1951	1966	D
607	GVH 807	BUT9641T	EE 150	E Lancs	72	1953	1966	
608	GVH 808	BUT9641T	EE 150	E Lancs	72	1953	1966	
609	GVH 809	BUT9641T	EE 150	E Lancs	72	1953	1966	
610	GVH 810	BUT9641T	EE 150	E Lancs	72	1953	1966	
611	GVH 811	BUT9641T	EE 150	E Lancs	72	1953	1966	
612	GVH 812	BUT9641T	EE 150	E Lancs	72	1953	1967	
613	GVH 813	BUT9641T	EE 150	E Lancs	72	1953	1967	
614	GVH 814	BUT9641T	EE 150	E Lancs	72	1953	1967	
615	GVH 815	BUT9641T	EE 150	E Lancs	72	1953	1967	D
616	GVH 816	BUT9641T	EE 150	E Lancs	72	1953	1966	D, A
617	GVH 817	BUT9641T	EE 150	E Lancs	72	1953	1967	D
618	GVH 818	BUT9641T	EE 150	E Lancs	72	1954	1967	D
619	KVH 219	BUT9641T	EE 150	E Lancs	72	1957	1968	P
620	KVH 220	BUT9641T	EE 150	E Lancs	72	1956	1968	
621	KVH 221	BUT9641T	EE 150	E Lancs	72	1956	1968	
622	KVH 222	BUT9641T	EE 150	E Lancs	72	1956	1968	
623	KVH 223	BUT9641T	EE 150	E Lancs	72	1956	1968	H
624	KVH 224	BUT9641T	EE 150	E Lancs	72	1956	1968	
625	KVH 225	BUT9641T	EE 150	E Lancs	72	1956	1967	D, A
626	KVH 226	BUT9641T	EE 150	E Lancs	72	1956	1968	D
627	KVH 227	BUT9641T	EE 150	E Lancs	72	1956	1968	
628	KVH 228	BUT9641T	EE 150	E Lancs	72	1956	1968	
629	KVH 229	BUT9641T	EE 150	E Lancs	72	1956	1968	
630	KVH 930	BUT9641T	EE 150	E Lancs	72	1956	1968	
631	PVH 931	S S7	MV 150	E Lancs	72	1959	1968	P
632	PVH 932	S S7	MV 150	E Lancs	72	1959	1968	
633	PVH 933	S S7	MV 150	E Lancs	72	1959	1968	
634	PVH 934	S S7	MV 150	E Lancs	72	1959	1967	F, A
635	PVH 935	S S7	MV 150	E Lancs	72	1959	1968	
636	PVH 936	S S7	MV 150	E Lancs	72	1959	1967	
637	PVH 937	S S7	MV 150	E Lancs	72	1959	1968	
638	PVH 938	S S7	MV 150	E Lancs	72	1959	1968	
639	PVH 939	S S7	MV 150	E Lancs	72	1959	1968	G
640	PVH 940	S S7	MV 150	E Lancs	72	1959	1968	

Abbreviations:

AEC	Associated Equipment Company
BTH	British Thomson-Houston
BUT	British United Traction
EE	English Electric
EL (or E Lancs)	East Lancashire Coachbuilders
K	Karrier
MV	Metropolitan Vickers
PR	Park Royal
RSJ	Ransomes, Simms and Jeffries
Ro	Roe
S	Sunbeam
SC	Seating capacity

Right–hand column notes:

A	Prematurely withdrawn due to accident damage
B	Sold to Reading Corporation Transport (see page 187)
C	Sold to Epsom and Ewell Council (see page 190)
D	Stored out of service from November 1961 to November 1962
E	The East Lancashire bodies from nos 556, 557, 561 and 563 were transferred in 1963 to nos 586, 587, 591 and 592 respectively.
F	The last trolleybus to be given a full repaint (1965).
G	The last trolleybus to be given a full overhaul (1966).
H	Fitted with illuminations in July 1968 as the official 'Last Trolleybus'.
P	Preserved in working order at The Trolleybus Museum, Sandtoft, Lincs.
Pc	Preserved (chassis only) at the Trolleybus Museum, Sandtoft, Lincs.
R	Rebuild (ie rebodied), make of replacement body and year shown. (Roe bodies on pre-war chassis seated 66, all other rebodies – 72).

Other notes

All trolleybuses had three axles and were 7 feet 6 inches wide.
Fleet nos. from 431 upwards had coasting and run-back brakes.
Fleet nos. up to 592 had regenerative braking.
All vehicles, except for metal framed no. 431, had high voltage interior lighting.
No vehicle was fitted with traction batteries.

Numerically Huddersfield's last trolleybus was no.640, which entered service on Christmas Eve, 1959. This pleasant scene in St George's Square shows the vehicle when still quite new. (H. Luff / Online Transport Archive)

HUDDERSFIELD CORPORATION TRANSPORT
Town Centre Trolleybus Wiring

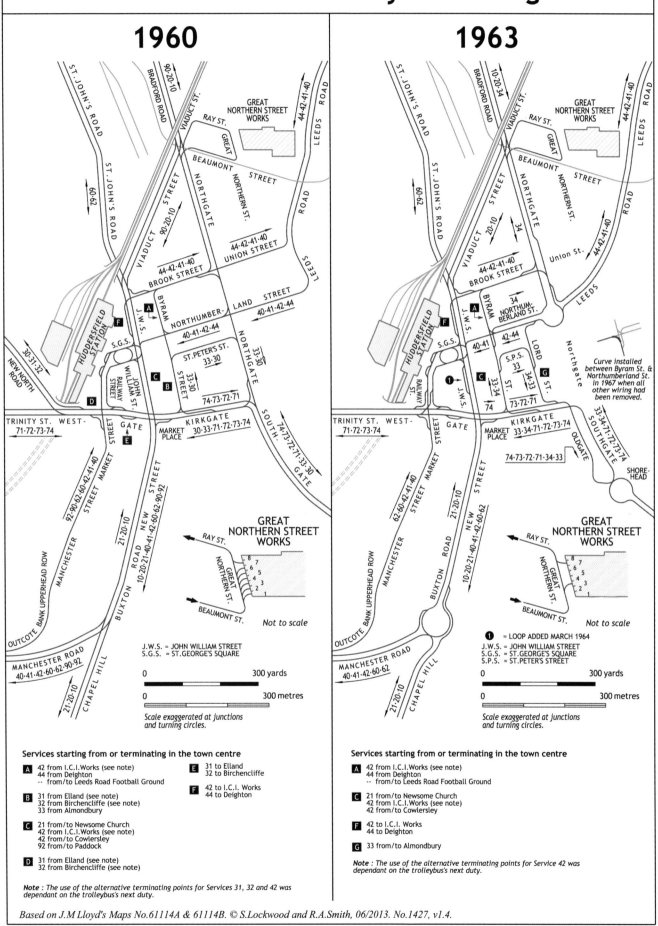

1960

1963

Services starting from or terminating in the town centre (1960)

A 42 from I.C.I.Works (see note)
44 from Deighton
-- from/to Leeds Road Football Ground

B 31 from Elland (see note)
32 from Birchencliffe (see note)
33 from Almondbury

C 21 from/to Newsome Church
42 from I.C.I.Works (see note)
42 from/to Cowlersley
92 from/to Paddock

D 31 from Elland (see note)
32 from Birchencliffe (see note)

E 31 to Elland
32 to Birchencliffe

F 42 to I.C.I. Works
44 to Deighton

Note : The use of the alternative terminating points for Services 31, 32 and 42 was dependant on the trolleybus's next duty.

Services starting from or terminating in the town centre (1963)

A 42 from I.C.I.Works (see note)
44 from Deighton
-- from/to Leeds Road Football Ground

C 21 from/to Newsome Church
42 from I.C.I.Works (see note)
42 from/to Cowlersley

F 42 to I.C.I. Works
44 to Deighton

G 33 from/to Almondbury

Note : The use of the alternative terminating points for Service 42 was dependant on the trolleybus's next duty.

① = LOOP ADDED MARCH 1964
J.W.S. = JOHN WILLIAM STREET
S.G.S. = ST.GEORGE'S SQUARE
S.P.S. = ST.PETER'S STREET

Curve installed between Byram St. & Northumberland St. in 1967 when all other wiring had been removed.

J.W.S. = JOHN WILLIAM STREET
S.G.S. = ST.GEORGE'S SQUARE

Based on J.M Lloyd's Maps No.61114A & 61114B. © S.Lockwood and R.A.Smith, 06/2013. No.1427, v1.4.

203

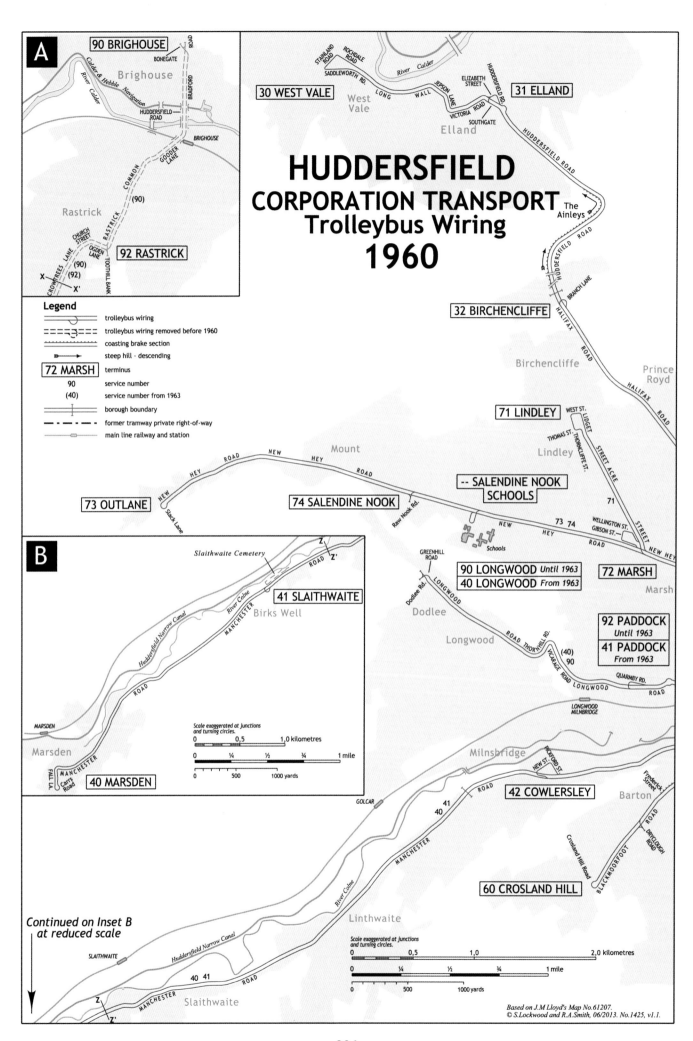

HUDDERSFIELD
CORPORATION TRANSPORT
Trolleybus Wiring
1960

The Ainleys

A

90 BRIGHOUSE

BONEGATE

Brighouse

River Calder

Calder & Hebble Navigation

HUDDERSFIELD ROAD

BRADFORD ROAD

BRIGHOUSE

Rastrick

GOODER LANE

COMMON

(90)

RASTRICK

CHURCH STREET

OGDEN LANE

TOOTHILL BANK

CROWTREES LANE

(90)
(92)

X

X'

92 RASTRICK

Legend

trolleybus wiring	
trolleybus wiring removed before 1960	
coasting brake section	
steep hill - descending	
72 MARSH	terminus
90	service number
(40)	service number from 1963
	borough boundary
	former tramway private right-of-way
	main line railway and station

STAINLAND ROAD
ROCHDALE ROAD
SADDLEWORTH RD.

River Calder

30 WEST VALE

West Vale

LONG WALL

JEPSON LANE

ELIZABETH STREET

HUDDERSFIELD RD.

31 ELLAND

VICTORIA ROAD

SOUTHGATE

Elland

HUDDERSFIELD ROAD

32 BIRCHENCLIFFE

HUDDERSFIELD ROAD

BRANCH LANE

HALIFAX ROAD

Birchencliffe

Prince Royd

HALIFAX ROAD

71 LINDLEY

WEST ST.

LIDGET STREET

THOMAS ST.
THORNCLIFFE ST.

STREET ACRE

Lindley

-- SALENDINE NOOK SCHOOLS

71

Mount

NEW HEY ROAD

73 OUTLANE

NEW HEY ROAD

SLACK LANE

74 SALENDINE NOOK

Raw Nook Rd.

NEW HEY ROAD

73 74

WELLINGTON ST.
GIBSON ST.

STREET

NEW HEY

Schools

90 LONGWOOD *Until 1963*
40 LONGWOOD *From 1963*

72 MARSH

Marsh

GREENHILL ROAD

Dodlee Rd.

LONGWOOD ROAD

Dodlee

92 PADDOCK
Until 1963
41 PADDOCK
From 1963

Longwood

LONGWOOD ROAD
THORNHILL RD.

VICARAGE ROAD

(40)
90

QUARMBY RD.

LONGWOOD ROAD

B

Slaithwaite Cemetery

Z
Z'

ROAD

41 SLAITHWAITE

River Colne

MANCHESTER

Birks Well

Huddersfield Narrow Canal

ROAD

MARSDEN

Marsden

MANCHESTER

FALL LA.
Carrs Road

40 MARSDEN

Scale exaggerated at junctions and turning circles.

0   0,5   1,0 kilometres

0   ¼   ½   ¾   1 mile

0   500   1000 yards

LONGWOOD MILNBRIDGE

Milnsbridge

PICKFORD ST.

NEW ST.

ROAD

42 COWLERSLEY

Barton

FREDERICK STREET

GOLCAR

41
40

MANCHESTER ROAD

River Colne

Linthwaite

Crosland Hill Road

BLACKMOORFOOT

DRYCLOUGH ROAD

60 CROSLAND HILL

Continued on Inset B at reduced scale

SLAITHWAITE

Huddersfield Narrow Canal

40 41

MANCHESTER ROAD

Slaithwaite

Z
Z'

Scale exaggerated at junctions and turning circles.

0   0,5   1,0   2,0 kilometres

0   ¼   ½   ¾   1 mile

0   500   1000 yards

Based on J.M Lloyd's Map No.61207.
© S.Lockwood and R.A.Smith, 06/2013. No.1425, v1.1.

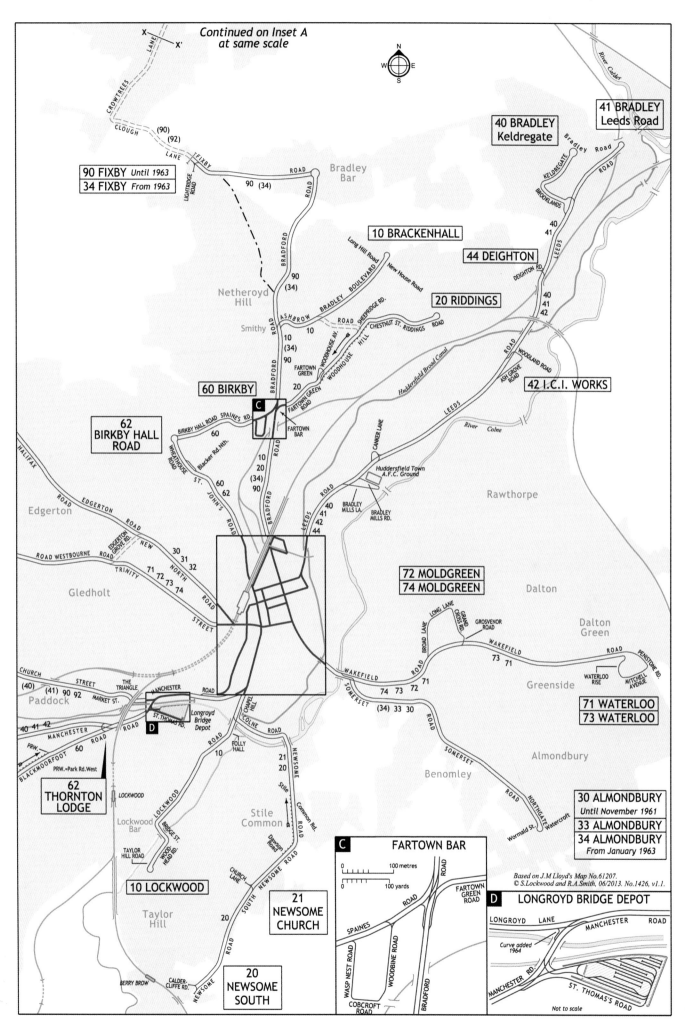

Continued on Inset A at same scale

X X'
CROWTREES
LANE
CLOUGH (90)
(92)
FIXBY LANE

90 FIXBY Until 1963
34 FIXBY From 1963

90 (34)
BRADFORD ROAD
Bradley Bar

40 BRADLEY Keldregate
41 BRADLEY Leeds Road

River Calder
Bradley Road
KELDREGATE
BROOKLANDS
LEEDS ROAD

40
41

10 BRACKENHALL

Long Hill Road
New House Road
BRADLEY BOULEVARD

44 DEIGHTON

DEIGHTON RD.

40
41
42

90 (34)
Netheroyd Hill

ASHBROW ROAD
SHEEPRIDGE RD.
Chestnut St. Riddings ROAD

20 RIDDINGS

Smithy
10
10 (34)
90
20
FARTOWN GREEN
FARTOWN GREEN ROAD
WOODHOUSE AV.
WOODHOUSE HILL

Huddersfield Broad Canal

WOODLAND ROAD
ASH GROVE ROAD

42 I.C.I. WORKS

60 BIRKBY

BIRKBY HALL ROAD
SPAINE'S RD.
C
FARTOWN BAR

62 BIRKBY HALL ROAD

WHEATHOUSE ROAD
Blacker Rd. Nth.
60
60
62
10
20
(34)
90

BRADFORD ROAD

LEEDS ROAD
CANKER LANE
River Colne

Rawthorpe

HALIFAX ROAD
Edgerton
EDGERTON ROAD
ST. JOHN'S ROAD

Huddersfield Town A.F.C. Ground

BRADLEY MILLS LA.
BRADLEY MILLS RD.

40
41
42
44

Dalton

ROAD WESTBOURNE ROAD
EDGERTON GROVE RD.
NEW NORTH ROAD
TRINITY
30 31 32
71 72 73 74

72 MOLDGREEN
74 MOLDGREEN

Dalton Green

Gledholt

LONG LANE
BROAD LANE
GRAND CROSS RD.
GROSVENOR ROAD
WAKEFIELD ROAD
73 71
PENISTONE RD.

CHURCH STREET
(40)
(41) 90 92
THE TRIANGLE
MARKET ST.
MANCHESTER ROAD
ST. THOMAS RD.
D
Longroyd Bridge Depot

71
WAKEFIELD ROAD
74 73 72
SOMERSET ROAD
(34) 33 30

Waterloo Rise
MITCHELL AVENUE

Greenside

71 WATERLOO
73 WATERLOO

Paddock
40 41 42
MANCHESTER ROAD
PRW.
BLACKMOORFOOT ROAD
PRW.=Park Rd.West
60

62 THORNTON LODGE

LOCKWOOD
TAYLOR HILL ROAD
Lockwood Bar
BRIDGE ST.
WOOL HEAD RD.

CHAPEL HILL
COLNE ROAD
FOLLY HALL
10
21
20
NEWSOME ROAD
Stile
Common Rd.
Dawson Road

Stile Common

SOMERSET ROAD
NORTHGATE ROAD
Almondbury
Benomley

Wormald St.
Watercroft

30 ALMONDBURY Until November 1961
33 ALMONDBURY
34 ALMONDBURY From January 1963

10 LOCKWOOD

CHURCH LANE
SOUTH NEWSOME ROAD

Taylor Hill

BERRY BROW
CALDER-CLIFFE RD.
NEWSOME ROAD

21 NEWSOME CHURCH

20 NEWSOME SOUTH

C **FARTOWN BAR**

0 ___ 100 metres
0 ___ 100 yards

SPAINES ROAD
WASP NEST ROAD
WOODBINE ROAD
BRADFORD ROAD
FARTOWN GREEN ROAD
COBCROFT ROAD

Based on J.M Lloyd's Map No.61207.
© S.Lockwood and R.A.Smith, 06/2013. No.1426, v1.1.

D **LONGROYD BRIDGE DEPOT**

LONGROYD LANE
MANCHESTER ROAD
Curve added 1964
MANCHESTER RD.
ST. THOMAS'S ROAD
Not to scale

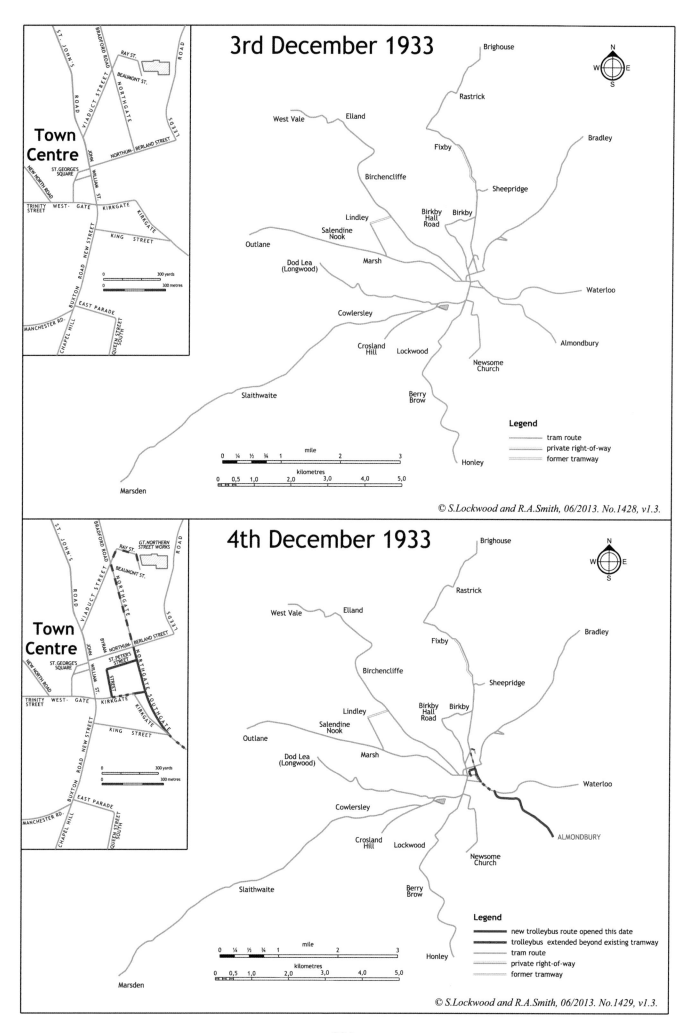

3rd December 1933

Town Centre

Legend
tram route
private right-of-way
former tramway

© S.Lockwood and R.A.Smith, 06/2013. No.1428, v1.3.

4th December 1933

Town Centre

Legend
new trolleybus route opened this date
trolleybus extended beyond existing tramway
tram route
private right-of-way
former tramway

© S.Lockwood and R.A.Smith, 06/2013. No.1429, v1.3.

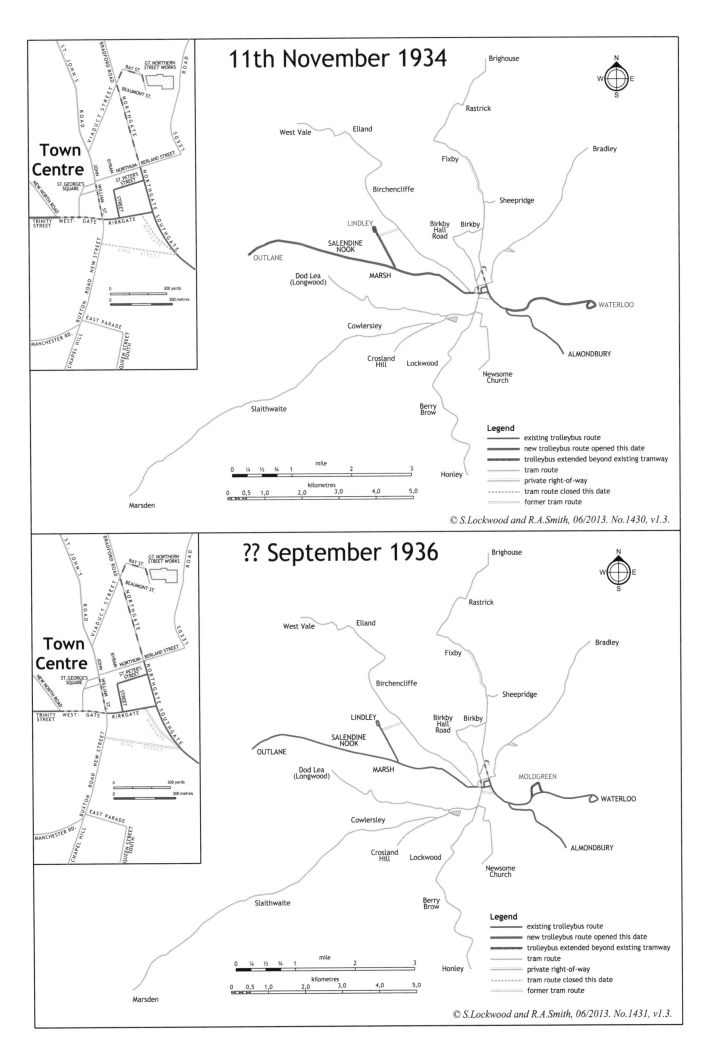

11th November 1934

Town Centre

Brighouse

Rastrick

West Vale   Elland

Bradley

Fixby

Birchencliffe

Sheepridge

LINDLEY

SALENDINE NOOK

Birkby Hall Road   Birkby

OUTLANE

MARSH

Dod Lea (Longwood)

WATERLOO

Cowlersley

ALMONDBURY

Crosland Hill   Lockwood

Newsome Church

Slaithwaite

Berry Brow

Legend

⎯⎯ existing trolleybus route
⎯⎯ new trolleybus route opened this date
▬▬ trolleybus extended beyond existing tramway
···· tram route
···· private right-of-way
---- tram route closed this date
···· former tram route

Honley

Marsden

mile 0 ¼ ½ ¾ 1 2 3
kilometres 0 0,5 1,0 2,0 3,0 4,0 5,0

© S.Lockwood and R.A.Smith, 06/2013. No.1430, v1.3.

?? September 1936

Town Centre

Brighouse

Rastrick

West Vale   Elland

Bradley

Fixby

Birchencliffe

Sheepridge

LINDLEY

Birkby Hall Road   Birkby

SALENDINE NOOK

OUTLANE

MARSH

Dod Lea (Longwood)

MOLDGREEN

WATERLOO

Cowlersley

ALMONDBURY

Crosland Hill   Lockwood

Newsome Church

Slaithwaite

Berry Brow

Legend

⎯⎯ existing trolleybus route
⎯⎯ new trolleybus route opened this date
▬▬ trolleybus extended beyond existing tramway
···· tram route
···· private right-of-way
---- tram route closed this date
···· former tram route

Honley

Marsden

mile 0 ¼ ½ ¾ 1 2 3
kilometres 0 0,5 1,0 2,0 3,0 4,0 5,0

© S.Lockwood and R.A.Smith, 06/2013. No.1431, v1.3.

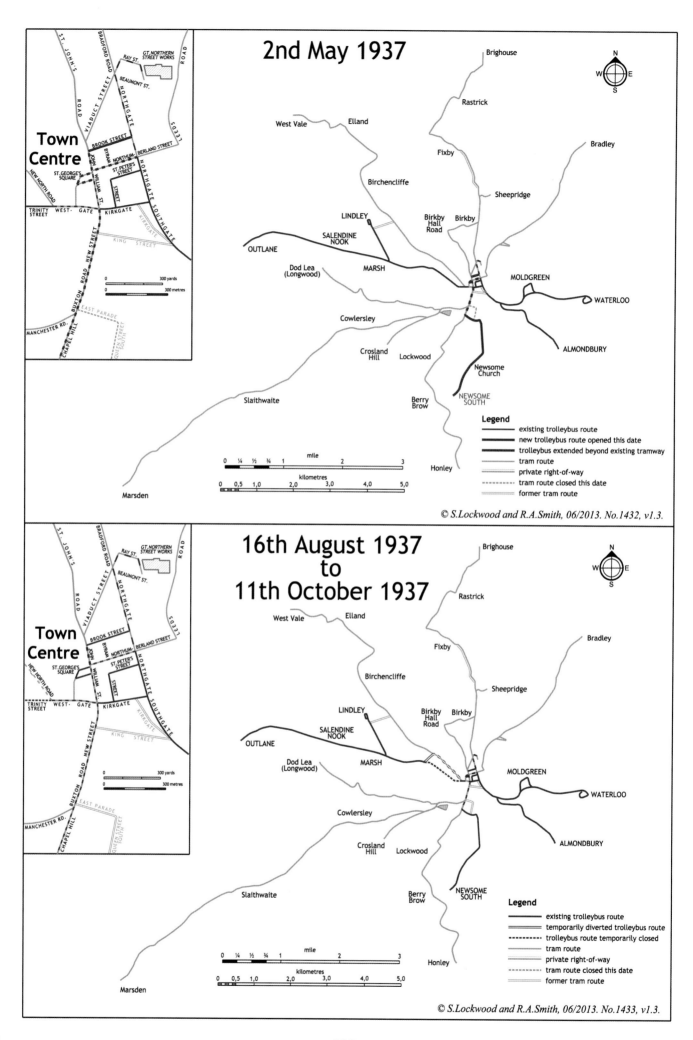

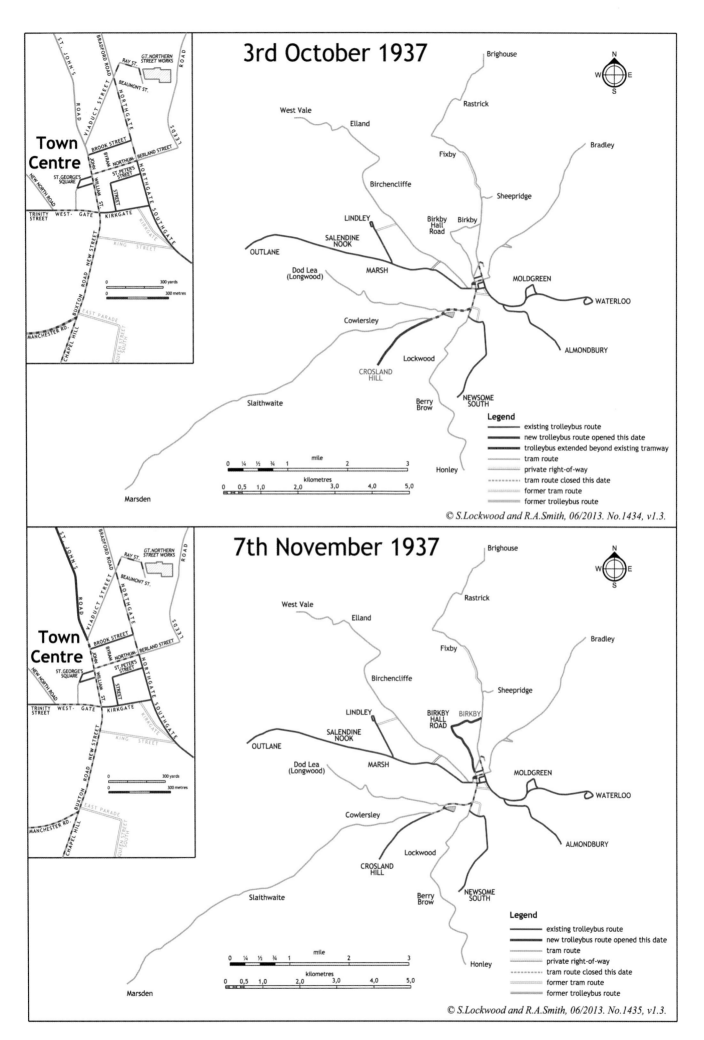

3rd October 1937

Town Centre

Legend
— existing trolleybus route
— new trolleybus route opened this date
— trolleybus extended beyond existing tramway
— tram route
— private right-of-way
— tram route closed this date
— former tram route
— former trolleybus route

© S.Lockwood and R.A.Smith, 06/2013. No.1434, v1.3.

7th November 1937

Town Centre

Legend
— existing trolleybus route
— new trolleybus route opened this date
— tram route
— private right-of-way
— tram route closed this date
— former tram route
— former trolleybus route

© S.Lockwood and R.A.Smith, 06/2013. No.1435, v1.3.

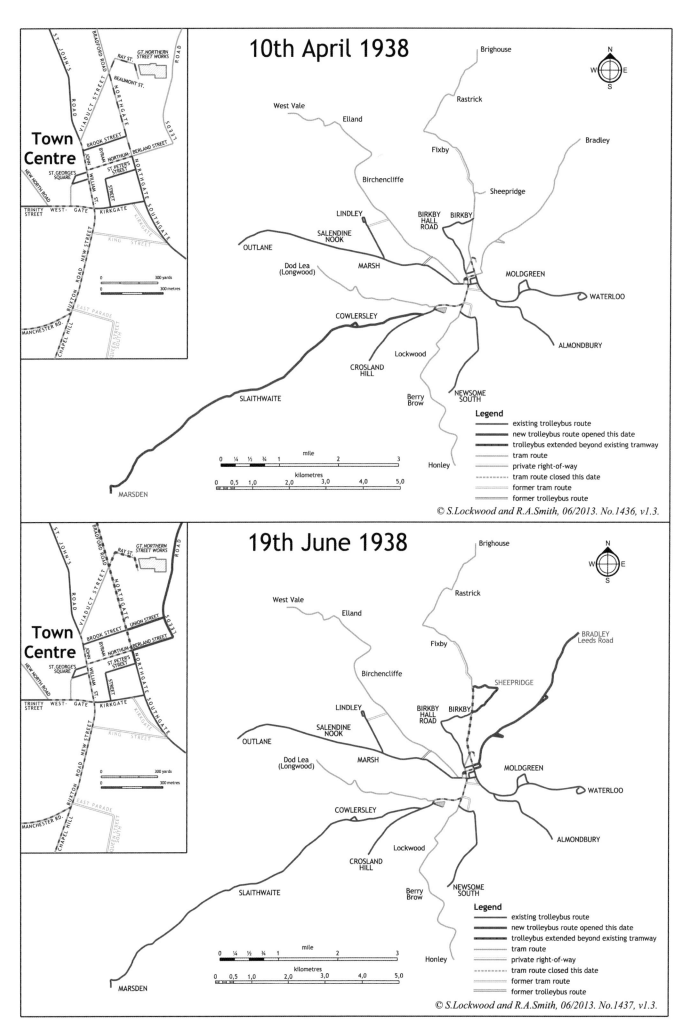

10th April 1938

Town Centre

Legend
existing trolleybus route
new trolleybus route opened this date
trolleybus extended beyond existing tramway
tram route
private right-of-way
tram route closed this date
former tram route
former trolleybus route

© S.Lockwood and R.A.Smith, 06/2013. No.1436, v1.3.

19th June 1938

Town Centre

Legend
existing trolleybus route
new trolleybus route opened this date
trolleybus extended beyond existing tramway
tram route
private right-of-way
tram route closed this date
former tram route
former trolleybus route

© S.Lockwood and R.A.Smith, 06/2013. No.1437, v1.3.

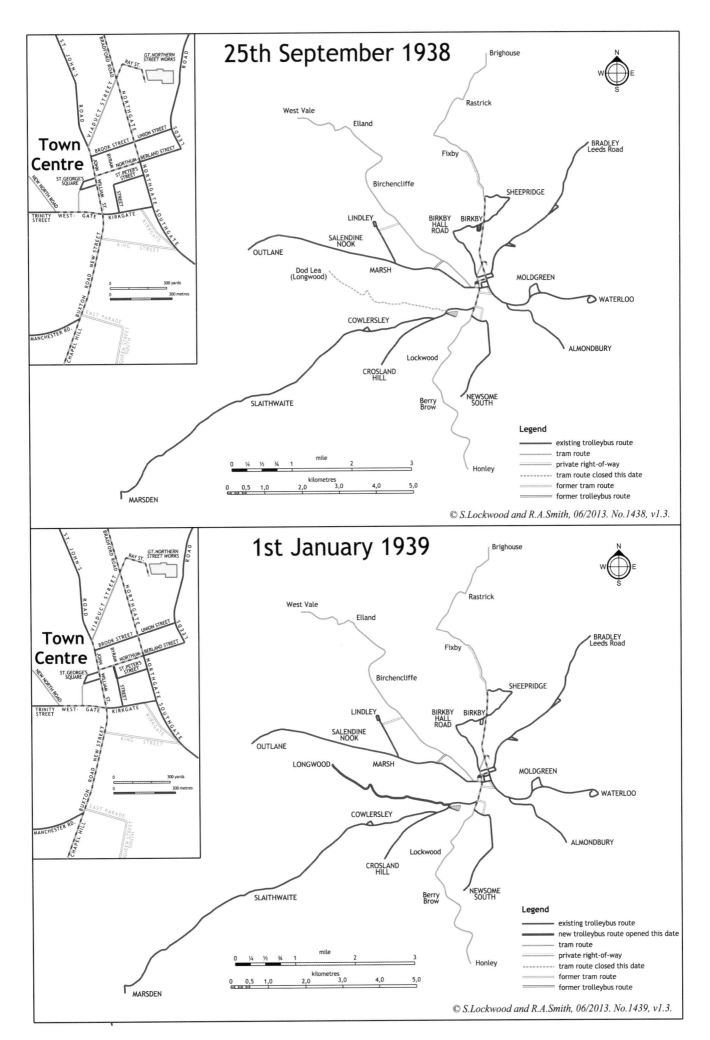

25th September 1938

Town Centre

Legend
— existing trolleybus route
— tram route
— private right-of-way
-- tram route closed this date
— former tram route
— former trolleybus route

© S.Lockwood and R.A.Smith, 06/2013. No.1438, v1.3.

1st January 1939

Town Centre

Legend
— existing trolleybus route
— new trolleybus route opened this date
— tram route
— private right-of-way
-- tram route closed this date
— former tram route
— former trolleybus route

© S.Lockwood and R.A.Smith, 06/2013. No.1439, v1.3.

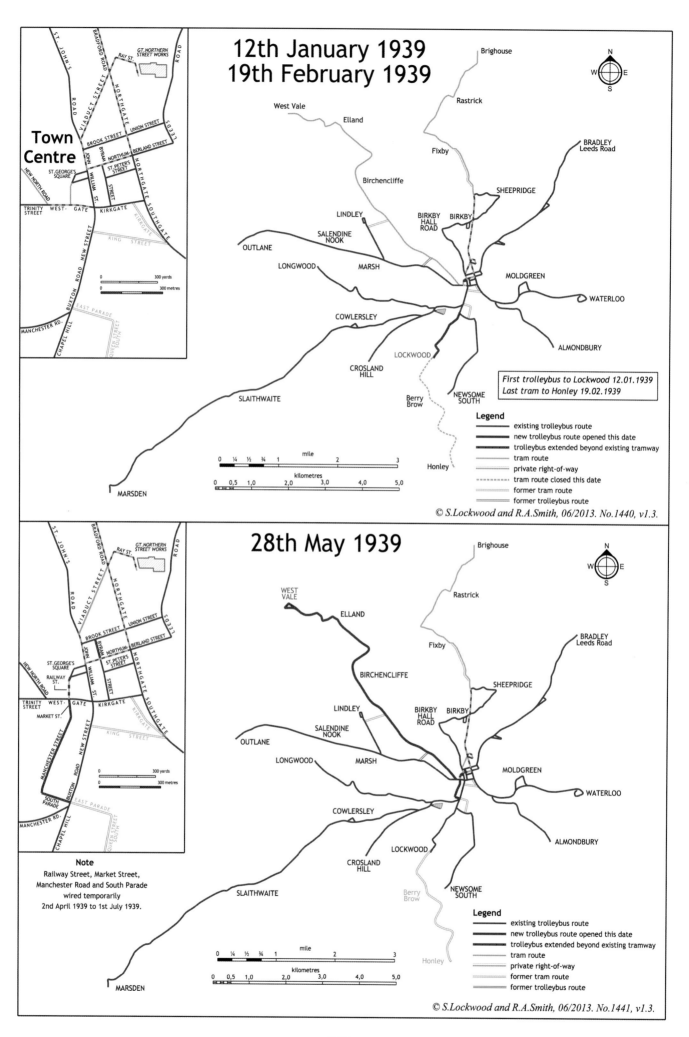

12th January 1939
19th February 1939

Town Centre

Brighouse

West Vale

Elland

Rastrick

Fixby

BRADLEY Leeds Road

Birchencliffe

SHEEPRIDGE

LINDLEY

SALENDINE NOOK

BIRKBY HALL ROAD

BIRKBY

OUTLANE

MARSH

LONGWOOD

MOLDGREEN

WATERLOO

COWLERSLEY

LOCKWOOD

ALMONDBURY

CROSLAND HILL

Berry Brow

NEWSOME SOUTH

SLAITHWAITE

Honley

First trolleybus to Lockwood 12.01.1939
Last tram to Honley 19.02.1939

MARSDEN

Legend

— existing trolleybus route
— new trolleybus route opened this date
— trolleybus extended beyond existing tramway
— tram route
— private right-of-way
-- tram route closed this date
— former tram route
— former trolleybus route

© S.Lockwood and R.A.Smith, 06/2013. No.1440, v1.3.

28th May 1939

Brighouse

WEST VALE

ELLAND

Rastrick

Fixby

BRADLEY Leeds Road

BIRCHENCLIFFE

SHEEPRIDGE

LINDLEY

SALENDINE NOOK

BIRKBY HALL ROAD

BIRKBY

OUTLANE

MARSH

LONGWOOD

MOLDGREEN

WATERLOO

COWLERSLEY

LOCKWOOD

ALMONDBURY

CROSLAND HILL

Berry Brow

NEWSOME SOUTH

SLAITHWAITE

Honley

Note
Railway Street, Market Street,
Manchester Road and South Parade
wired temporarily
2nd April 1939 to 1st July 1939.

MARSDEN

Legend

— existing trolleybus route
— new trolleybus route opened this date
— trolleybus extended beyond existing tramway
— tram route
— private right-of-way
— former tram route
— former trolleybus route

© S.Lockwood and R.A.Smith, 06/2013. No.1441, v1.3.

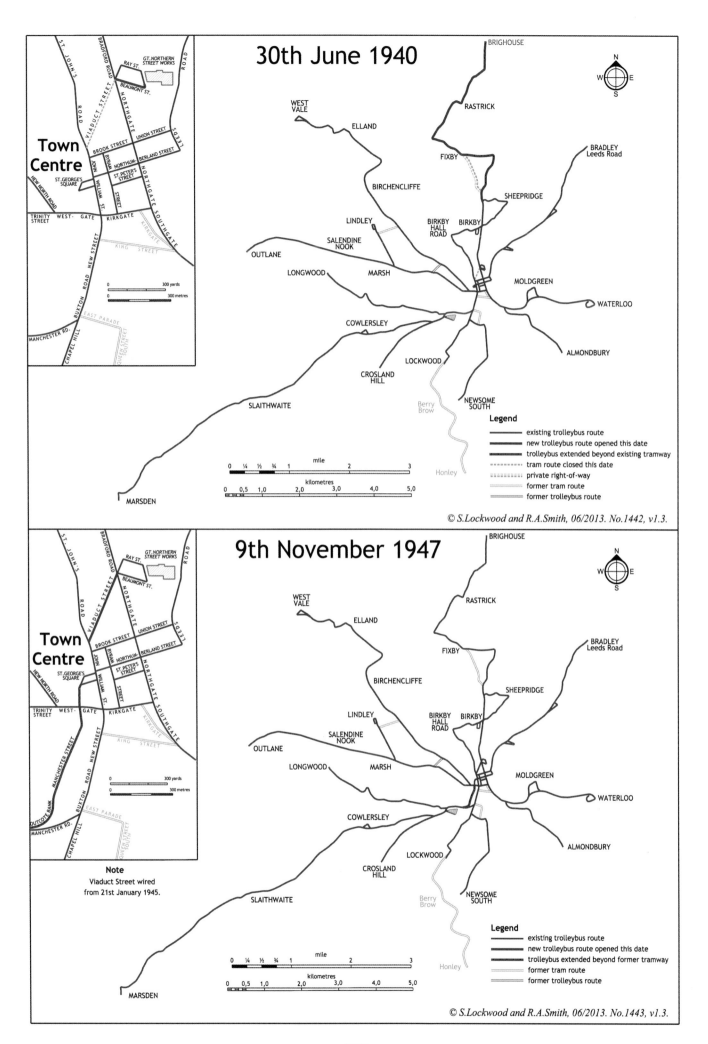

30th June 1940

Town Centre

Legend

— existing trolleybus route
— new trolleybus route opened this date
— trolleybus extended beyond existing tramway
‑ ‑ tram route closed this date
════ private right-of-way
════ former tram route
— former trolleybus route

© S.Lockwood and R.A.Smith, 06/2013. No.1442, v1.3.

BRIGHOUSE
RASTRICK
WEST VALE
ELLAND
FIXBY
BRADLEY Leeds Road
BIRCHENCLIFFE
SHEEPRIDGE
LINDLEY
BIRKBY HALL ROAD
BIRKBY
SALENDINE NOOK
OUTLANE
LONGWOOD
MARSH
MOLDGREEN
COWLERSLEY
WATERLOO
LOCKWOOD
ALMONDBURY
CROSLAND HILL
Berry Brow
NEWSOME SOUTH
SLAITHWAITE
Honley
MARSDEN

ST. JOHN'S ROAD
BRADFORD ROAD
RAY ST
GT.NORTHERN STREET WORKS
BEAUMONT ST.
VIADUCT STREET
NORTHGATE
LEEDS ROAD
BROOK STREET
UNION STREET
JOHN ST
BYRAM
NORTHUM
BERLAND STREET
ST.GEORGE'S SQUARE
WILLIAM ST.
ST. PETER'S STREET
NEW NORTH ROAD
TRINITY STREET
WEST-GATE
KIRKGATE
NORTHGATE SOUTHGATE
KIRKGATE
NEW STREET
KING STREET
BUXTON ROAD
CHAPEL HILL
EAST PARADE
MANCHESTER RD.
QUEEN STREET SOUTH

0   ¼ ½ ¾ 1   2   3   mile
0 0,5 1,0   2,0   3,0   4,0   5,0 kilometres

300 yards
300 metres

9th November 1947

Town Centre

Note
Viaduct Street wired from 21st January 1945.

Legend

— existing trolleybus route
— new trolleybus route opened this date
— trolleybus extended beyond former tramway
════ former tram route
— former trolleybus route

© S.Lockwood and R.A.Smith, 06/2013. No.1443, v1.3.

BRIGHOUSE
RASTRICK
WEST VALE
ELLAND
FIXBY
BRADLEY Leeds Road
BIRCHENCLIFFE
SHEEPRIDGE
LINDLEY
BIRKBY HALL ROAD
BIRKBY
SALENDINE NOOK
OUTLANE
LONGWOOD
MARSH
MOLDGREEN
COWLERSLEY
WATERLOO
LOCKWOOD
ALMONDBURY
CROSLAND HILL
Berry Brow
NEWSOME SOUTH
SLAITHWAITE
Honley
MARSDEN

ST. JOHN'S ROAD
BRADFORD ROAD
RAY ST
GT.NORTHERN STREET WORKS
BEAUMONT ST.
VIADUCT STREET
NORTHGATE
LEEDS ROAD
BROOK STREET
UNION STREET
JOHN ST
BYRAM
NORTHUM
BERLAND STREET
ST.GEORGE'S SQUARE
WILLIAM ST.
ST. PETER'S STREET
NEW NORTH ROAD
TRINITY STREET
WEST-GATE
KIRKGATE
NORTHGATE SOUTHGATE
KIRKGATE
NEW STREET
KING STREET
BUXTON ROAD
CHAPEL HILL
EAST PARADE
MANCHESTER STREET
OUTCOTE BANK
MANCHESTER RD.
QUEEN STREET SOUTH

0   ¼ ½ ¾ 1   2   3   mile
0 0,5 1,0   2,0   3,0   4,0   5,0 kilometres

300 yards
300 metres

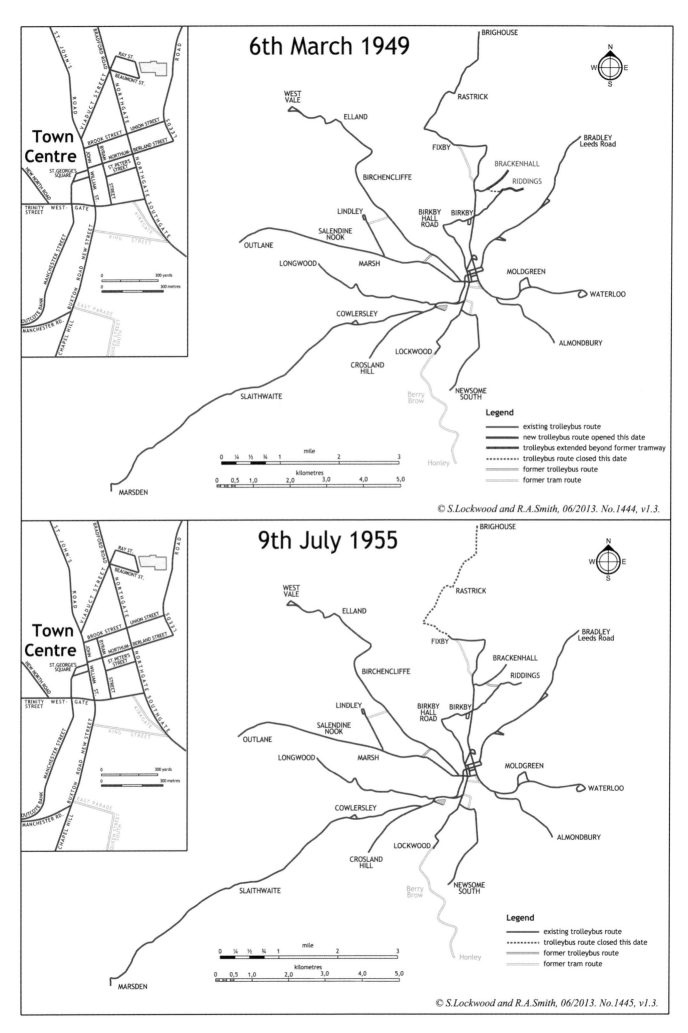

© S.Lockwood and R.A.Smith, 06/2013. No.1444, v1.3.

© S.Lockwood and R.A.Smith, 06/2013. No.1445, v1.3.

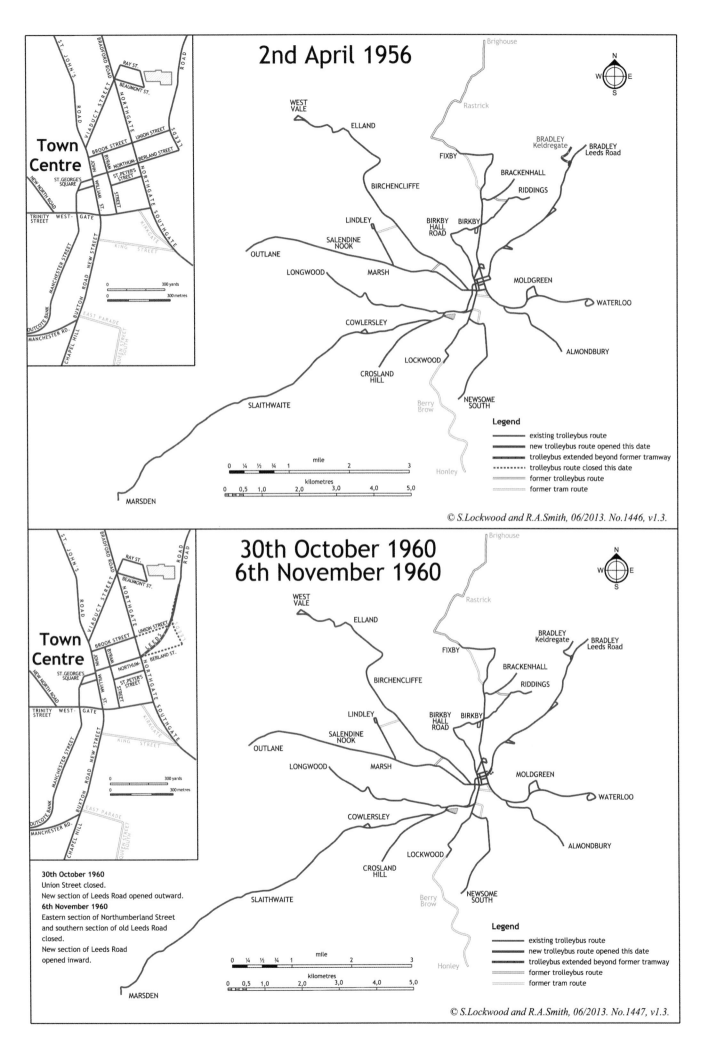

2nd April 1956

Town Centre

Legend
- existing trolleybus route
- new trolleybus route opened this date
- trolleybus extended beyond former tramway
- trolleybus route closed this date
- former trolleybus route
- former tram route

© S.Lockwood and R.A.Smith, 06/2013. No.1446, v1.3.

30th October 1960
6th November 1960

Town Centre

30th October 1960
Union Street closed.
New section of Leeds Road opened outward.

6th November 1960
Eastern section of Northumberland Street and southern section of old Leeds Road closed.
New section of Leeds Road opened inward.

Legend
- existing trolleybus route
- new trolleybus route opened this date
- trolleybus extended beyond former tramway
- former trolleybus route
- former tram route

© S.Lockwood and R.A.Smith, 06/2013. No.1447, v1.3.

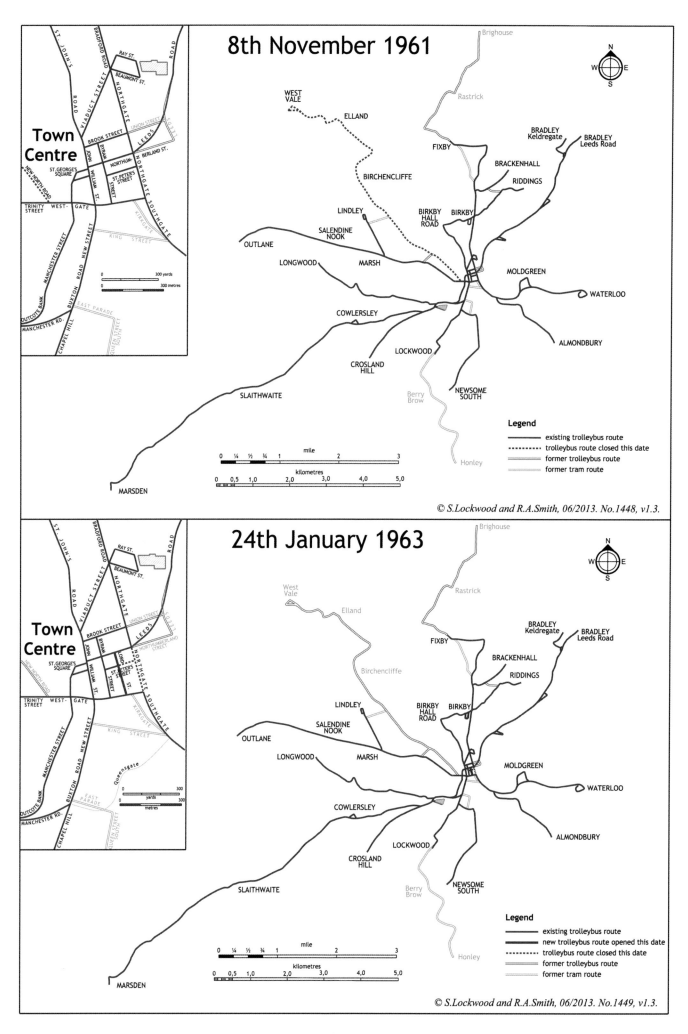

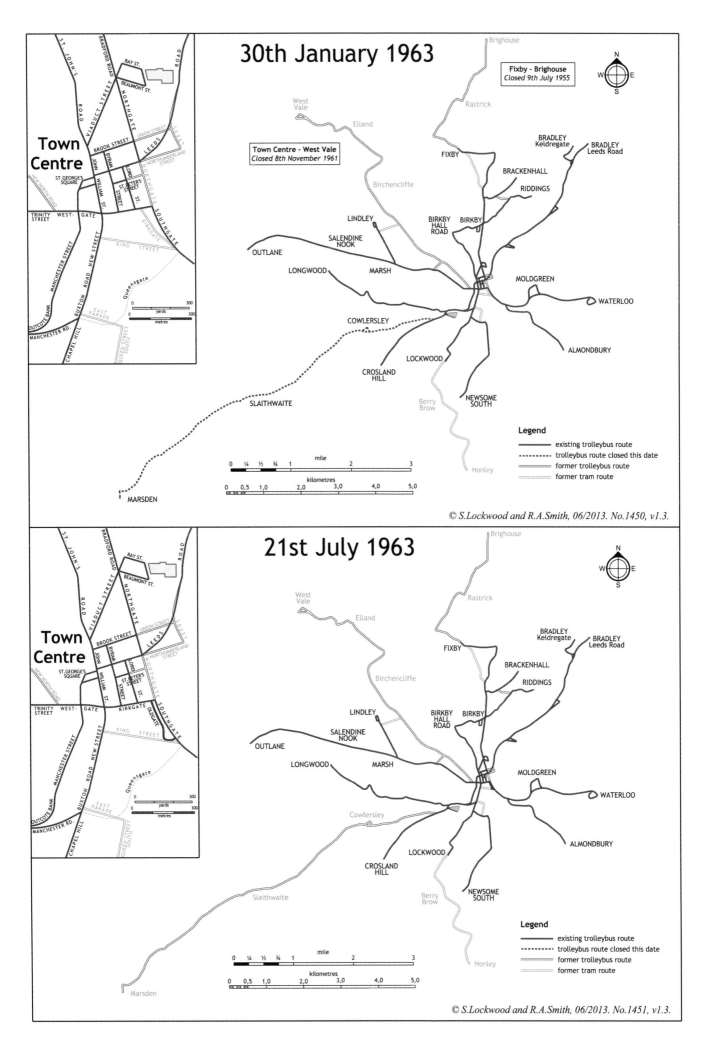

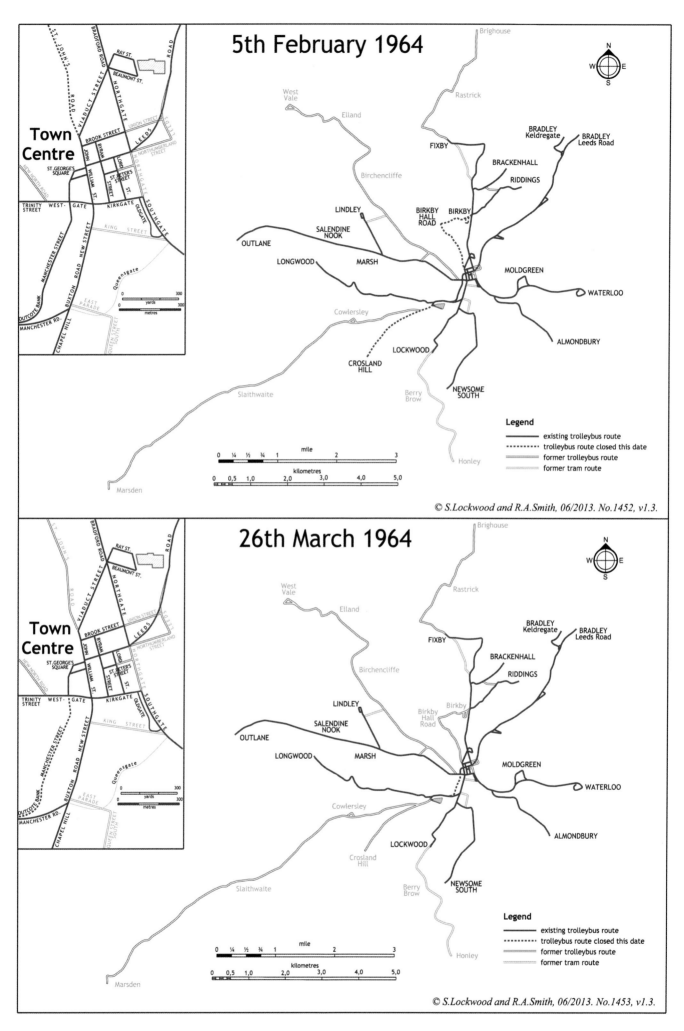

© S.Lockwood and R.A.Smith, 06/2013. No.1452, v1.3.

© S.Lockwood and R.A.Smith, 06/2013. No.1453, v1.3.

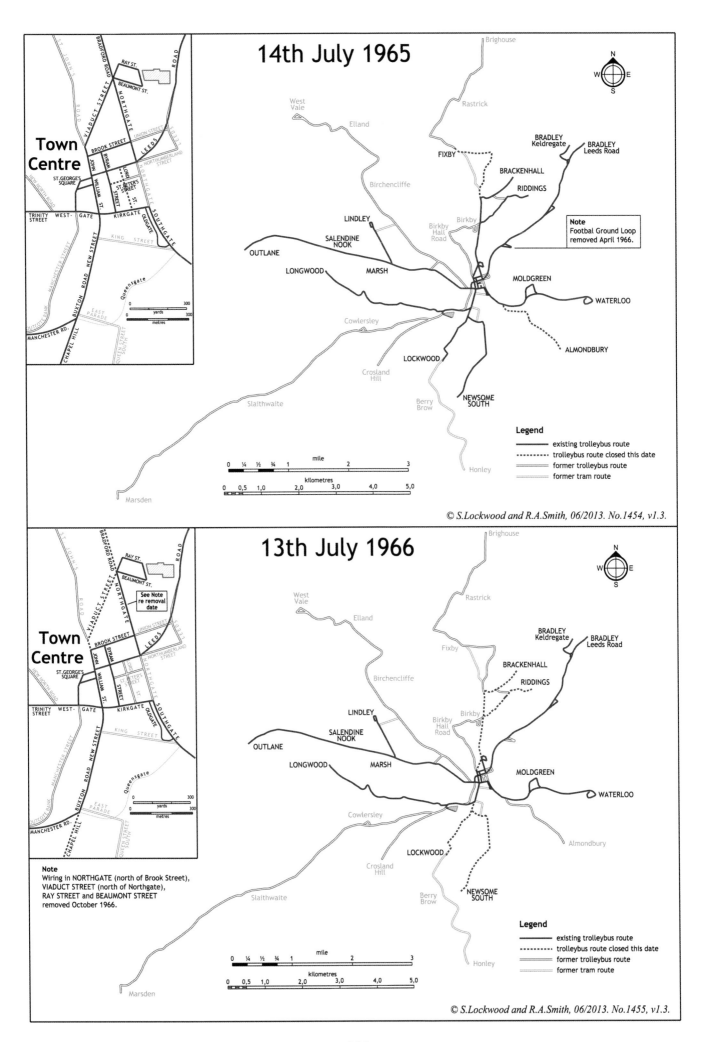

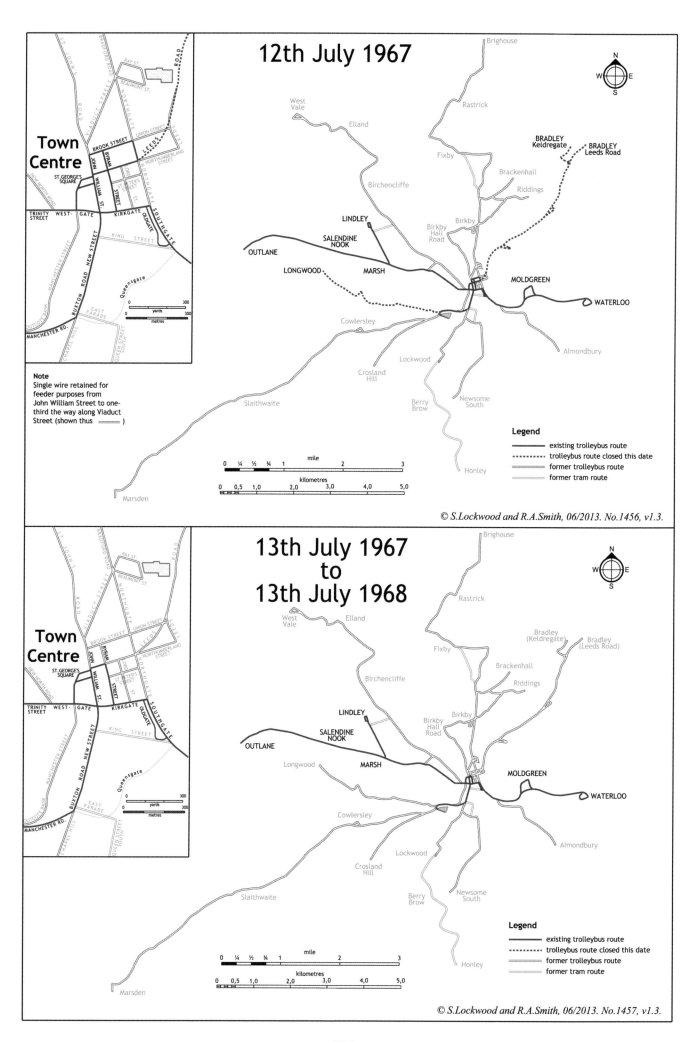

© S.Lockwood and R.A.Smith, 06/2013. No.1456, v1.3.

© S.Lockwood and R.A.Smith, 06/2013. No.1457, v1.3.

Ticket 1

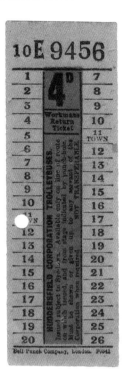

Ticket 2

Ticket 3

Ticket 4

Ticket 5

Ticket 6

Ticket 7

From 1933, trolleybus conductors issued tickets from ticket racks, these being punched by standard Bell Punches. The tickets bore the title 'Huddersfield Corporation Trackless Trolleys Vehicles' (ticket 1).

After the Second World War, the title on the tickets was changed to 'Huddersfield Corporation Trolleybuses' (ticket 2).

An experiment using two Willebrew ticket machines was made in 1944, but it was not until 1949 that the ticket punch system was superseded by Bell Punch 'Ultimate' ticket issuing machines. These were 5-unit models, and the design of ticket bore the title 'Huddersfield CPT. Each value of ticket had a separate colour. (ticket 3).

By the early 1960s the tickets simply bore the title 'Huddersfield', allowing stocks to be used on both Corporation and Joint Omnibus vehicles. (ticket 4, issued on trolleybus 616 in August 1965 following a fares increase – old stock was being used.)

In 1963 the tickets were re-designed to show a bold overprint of the fare value. (tickets 5 and 6 – the latter ticket was issued on the last trolleybus journey from Almondbury to town on 14th July 1965 – trolley no. 593.)

From 1967, the range of fares had increased and accordingly 6-unit Ultimate machines were introduced.

For the final trolleybus week in July 1968, all trolleybus conductors issued commemorative tickets from their Ultimate machines. (tickets 7 and 8). Ticket 22707 is an example of a 'married' issue of two 4d value tickets for an 8d fare. This was issued on no 629 on the last public service trolleybus journey on 13 July 1968, Outlane to town. 3d no 22110 was for the subsequent town to depot journey. The reverse of these tickets is also shown (ticket 9).

The guests travelling on no 623, the official 'Last Trolleybus', were issued with special card tickets. (ticket 10)

Ticket 10

Ticket 8

Ticket 9

County Borough of **HUDDERSFIELD**
PASSENGER TRANSPORT DEPT.

SOUVENIR TICKET

Commemorating the end of the Electrical
era of operation of Tramcars and
Trolleybuses.

14th. FEB. 1901 to 13th. JULY 1968

HUDDERSFIELD CORPORATION PASSENGER TRANSPORT DEPARTMENT

BIRKBY   No. 61

Sunday, April 5th, 1942, until further notice.

FROM TOWN.		FROM BIRKBY.	
MONDAY to FRIDAY.			
5.57 a.m. and every 10 min. until 7.37 a.m.	6.7 a.m. and every 10 min. until 7.17 a.m.		
7.37 a.m. ,, 5 ,, 8.57 a.m.	7.17 a.m. ,, 5 ,, 9.7 a.m.		
8.57 a.m. ,, 10 ,, 11.57 a.m.	9.7 a.m. ,, 10 ,, 12.7 p.m.		
11.57 a.m. ,, 5 ,, 4.42 p.m.	12.7 p.m. ,, 5 ,, 4.52 p.m.		
4.42 p.m. ,, 4 ,, 6.14 p.m.	4.52 p.m. ,, 4 ,, 5.56 p.m.		
6.17 p.m. ,, 5 ,, 7.47 p.m.	6.2 p.m. ,, 5 ,, 7.57 p.m.		
7.47 p.m. ,, 10 ,, 10.57 p.m.	7.57 p.m. ,, 10 ,, 11.7 p.m.		

SATURDAYS.

As Monday to Friday until 10.37 a.m., then	As Monday to Friday until 10.47 a.m., then		
10.37 a.m. and every 5 min. until 11.42 a.m.	10.47 a.m. and every 5 min. until 11.52 a.m.		
11.42 a.m. ,, 4 ,, 5.42 p.m.	11.52 a.m. ,, 4 ,, 5.52 p.m.		
5.47 p.m. ,, 5 ,, 10.57 p.m.	5.57 p.m. ,, 5 ,, 11.7 p.m.		

SUNDAYS.

7.22 a.m.	7.0 a.m., 7.30 a.m.		
7.55 a.m. and every 30 min. until 12.55 p.m.	8.15 a.m. and every 30 min. until 1.15 p.m.		
1.27 p.m. ,, 10 ,, 10.57 p.m.	1.37 p.m. ,, 10 ,, 11.7 p.m.		

H. MUSCROFT,
General Manager and Engineer.

April, 1942.

Alfred Jubb & Son, Ltd., Printers, Huddersfield.

HUDDERSFIELD CORPORATION PASSENGER TRANSPORT DEPARTMENT.

Lockwood Section   Service No. 50

REVISED TIME TABLE.

Monday, February 23rd, 1942, until further notice.

To LOCKWOOD.	From LOCKWOOD.
MONDAY TO FRIDAY.	
5.36 a.m. and every 12 minutes until 6.24 a.m.	5.50 a.m. and every 12 minutes until 6.38 a.m.
6.24 a.m. ,, 6 ,, 9.0 a.m.	6.38 a.m. ,, 6 ,, 9.2 a.m.
9.15 a.m. ,, 10 ,, 11.15 a.m.	9.10 a.m. ,, 10 ,, 11.30 a.m.
11.24 a.m. ,, 6 ,, 7.30 p.m.	11.38 a.m. ,, 6 ,, 7.44 p.m.
7.35 p.m. ,, 10 ,, 9.45 p.m.	7.50 p.m. ,, 10 ,, 10.0 p.m.
and 10.0 p.m.	and 10.14 p.m.

SATURDAYS.

As Monday to Friday until 10.55 a.m.	As Monday to Friday until 11.10 a.m.
11.6 a.m. and every 6 minutes until 10.0 p.m.	11.20 a.m. and every 6 minutes until 10.14 p.m.

SUNDAYS.

6.55 a.m. 7.55 a.m. 8.55 a.m.	7.5 a.m. 8.10 a.m. 9.10 a.m.
9.55 a.m. and every 30 minutes until 1.25 p.m.	10.10 a.m. and every 30 minutes until 1.40 p.m.
1.25 p.m. ,, 10 ,, 9.45 p.m.	1.40 p.m. ,, 10 ,, 10.0 p.m.
and 10.0 p.m.	and 10.14 p.m.

EXTRA CARS WILL BE RUN AT PEAK PERIODS ACCORDING TO TRAFFIC REQUIREMENTS.

Passenger Transport Offices,
February, 1942.

H. MUSCROFT,
General Manager and Engineer.

Wheatley, Dyson & Son, Printers, New Street, Huddersfield.

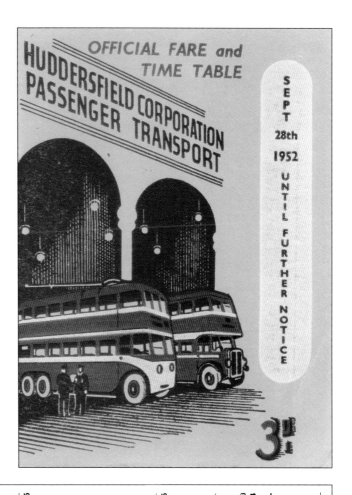

HUDDERSFIELD CORPORATION PASSENGER TRANSPORT DEPARTMENT

No. 90

BRIGHOUSE

Sunday, 2nd October, 1949, until further notice

MONDAY to FRIDAY

	a.m.	a.m.	a.m.	a.m.		p.m.	p.m.	p.m.	p.m.
Huddersfield (John Wm. St.)	5-0	5-15	5-30	5-45	And every 15 min. until	10-45	11-0	11-25	11-55
Lightridge Road	5-14	5-29	5-44	5-59		10-59	11-14	11-39	12-9
Ogden Lane	5-21	5-36	5-51	6-6		11-6	11-21		
Brighouse (Bonegate)	5-28	5-43	5-58	6-13		11-13	11-28		

	a.m.	a.m.	a.m.	a.m.		p.m.	p.m.	p.m.	p.m.
Brighouse (Bonegate)	5-33	5-48	6-3	6-18	And every 15 min. until	11-18	11-33		
Ogden Lane	5-40	5-55	6-10	6-25		11-25	11-40		
Lightridge Road	5-47	6-2	6-17	6-32		11-32	11-47	12-10	
Huddersfield (John Wm. St.)	6-1	6-16	6-31	6-46		11-46	12-1	12-10	12-24

SATURDAYS

	a.m.	a.m.	a.m.	a.m.		p.m.		p.m.	p.m.	p.m.
Huddersfield (John Wm. St.)	5-0	5-15	5-30	5-45	And every 15 min. until	10-30	And every 7½ min. until	11-0	11-25	11-55
Lightridge Road	5-14	5-29	5-44	5-59		10-44		11-14	11-39	12-9
Ogden Lane	5-21	5-36	5-51	6-6		10-51		11-21		
Brighouse (Bonegate)	5-28	5-43	5-58	6-13		10-58		11-28		

	a.m.	a.m.	a.m.	a.m.		p.m.		p.m.	p.m.	p.m.
Brighouse (Bonegate)	5-33	5-48	6-3	6-18	And every 15 min. until	11-3		11-33	11-40	
Ogden Lane	5-40	5-55	6-10	6-25		11-10		11-40	11-47	12-10
Lightridge Road	5-47	6-2	6-17	6-32		11-17		11-47		12-10
Huddersfield (John Wm. St.)	6-1	6-16	6-31	6-46		11-31		12-1		12-24

SUNDAYS

	a.m.	a.m.	a.m.		p.m.	p.m.		p.m.	p.m.	p.m.	p.m.
Huddersfield (John Wm. St.)	6-15	7-25	8-25	And every 30 mins. until	12-55	1-24	And every 12 min. until	1-57	11-0	11-25	11-55
Lightridge Road	6-29	7-39	8-39		1-9	1-38		2-4	11-14	11-39	12-9
Ogden Lane	6-36	7-46	8-46		1-16	1-45		2-11	11-21		
Brighouse (Bonegate)	6-43	7-53	8-53		1-23	1-52		2-25	11-28		

	a.m.	a.m.	a.m.		p.m.	p.m.		p.m.	p.m.	p.m.	a.m.
Brighouse (Bonegate)	6-45	8-15	8-55	And every 30 mins. until	1-25	1-57	And every 12 min. until	11-21	11-33		
Ogden Lane	6-52	8-22	9-2		1-32	2-4		11-28	11-40		
Lightridge Road	6-59	8-29	9-9		1-39	2-11		11-35	11-47	12-10	
Huddersfield (John Wm. St.)	7-13	8-43	9-23		1-53	2-25		11-49	12-1		12-24

H. MUSCROFT.
General Manager and Engineer.

THE ADVERTISER PRESS, LTD., PAGE STREET, HUDDERSFIELD.

FIXBY (Lightridge Road)

[Including Journeys on Brighouse (Route No. 90)]

Trolleybus Route No. 91

(Starts from St. George's Square)

Mins. Service	FROM TOWN	Mins. Service	FROM LIGHTRIDGE RD.
	MONDAY to FRIDAY		
	5.10 a.m.		
10	5.30 a.m. to 11.0 p.m.	10	5.54 a.m. to 11.34 p.m.
	11.25 p.m., 11.55 p.m.		11.40 p.m., 12.10 a.m.
	SATURDAY		
20	5.10 a.m. to 7.50 a.m.	20	5.54 a.m. to 8.14 a.m.
10	7.50 ,, ,, 11.0 p.m.	10	8.14 ,, ,, 11.34 p.m.
	11.25 p.m., 11.55 p.m.		11.40 p.m., 11.44 p.m., 12.10 a.m.
	SUNDAY		
	6.15 a.m., 7.25 a.m.		6.59 a.m., 8.29 a.m.
30	8.25 a.m. to 1.25 p.m.	30	9.09 a.m. to 1.39 p.m.
10	1.40 p.m. to 11.0 ,,	10	2.14 p.m. ,, 11.34 ,,
	11.25 p.m., 11.55 p.m.		11.40 p.m., 12.10 a.m.

BUSES ARRIVE
FIXBY (Lightridge Road)
14 mins. after the
above times.

BUSES ARRIVE
TOWN, 14 mins. after the
above times.

1952

MOLDGREEN

(Long Lane)

Trolleybus Routes No. 72 and 74

(Starts from Westgate)

Mins. Service	FROM TOWN	Mins. Service	FROM MOLDGREEN
	MONDAY to FRIDAY		
15	6.38 a.m. to 8.38 a.m.	15	6.52 a.m. to 8.52 a.m.
20	11.56 a.m. ,, 3.56 p.m. (A)	20	12.06 p.m. ,, 4.06 p.m. (B)
10	3.56 p.m. ,, 5.56 ,,	10	4.06 ,, ,, 6.06 ,,
	SATURDAY		
15	8.5 a.m. to 5.5 p.m.	15	8.16 a.m. to 5.16 p.m.
20*	5.16 p.m. ,, 10.56 ,,	20†	5.26 p.m., ,, 11.06 ,,
	SUNDAY		
	No Service		No Service

(A) On Wednesdays only until 1.36 p.m.

(B) On Wednesdays only until 1.46 p.m.

*No journey at 7.16 p.m.

†No journey at 7.26 p.m.

BUSES PASS
MOLDGREEN (Junction) 6 mins.
ARRIVE LONG LANE 8 mins.
after above times.

BUSES PASS
MOLDGREEN (Junction) 3 mins.
ARRIVE TOWN 9 mins.
after above times.

For other Buses between Town and Moldgreen (Junction), see Waterloo
Routes (71 and 73)

1961

HUDDERSFIELD CORPORATION
PASSENGER TRANSPORT

ALMONDBURY — FIXBY
ROUTE No. 34

Commencing Thursday, 31st January, 1963, the route between Huddersfield and Fixby will be linked with the Huddersfield-Almondbury route.

Route outwards to Fixby

Byram Street, Northumberland Street, Northgate, Bradford Road.

Route inwards from Fixby

Bradford Road, Northgate, Northumberland Street, Lord Street.

Starting Points in Town Centre

To Fixby
In Byram Street at passenger shelter.

To Almondbury
In Lord Street near junction with St. Peter's Street.

Stopping Places

All existing stops will be used. An additional stop will be placed in Northgate near the junction with Viaduct Street.

For details of time and fare tables, see over.

E. V. DYSON, M.I.Mech.E., A.M.I.E.E., A.M.Inst.T.
General Manager & Engineer.

EXTENSION OF SHEEPRIDGE AND WOODHOUSE TROLLEYBUS ROUTES

COMMENCING on SUNDAY, 6th MARCH, 1949, the SHEEPRIDGE (No. 10) Trolleybus Route will be diverted along BRADLEY BOULEVARD and the WOODHOUSE (No.20) Route diverted via Chestnut Street to RIDDINGS ROAD.

The operation of the services in Ash Brow Road, between Bradley Boulevard and Woodhouse Hill will be discontinued.

Copies of the Time Table and Fare Lists may be obtained from Conductors or from the Passenger Transport Offices.

Passenger Transport Offices.
Huddersfield.

H. MUSCROFT,
General Manager and Engineer.

Revised Linking of Cross - Town Trolley Bus Services

Commencing on **SUNDAY, NOV. 9th, 1947** the following alterations will be made in the linking of **CROSS-TOWN TROLLEY BUS SERVICES :**

LOCKWOOD will be linked with **SHEEPRIDGE**—Service No. **10**

LONGWOOD will be linked with **BRIGHOUSE**—Service No. **90**

Copies of the **REVISED TIME TABLES** to be operated on these routes may be obtained at the Passsenger Transport Offices

H. MUSCROFT
General Manager and Engineer

Passenger Transport Department
October 1947

226

LAST REQUESTS

It might be assumed that the choice of vehicle which performed the last trolleybus run on any particular route was entirely arbitrary. In most cases it was pure chance, and was probably decided by where the trolley in question was parked in the depot the previous evening.

On at least three instances, however, enthusiasts requested certain vehicles to perform the closing journey.

On the West Vale route closure of 8 November 1961, the youngest and eldest vehicles in service were requested, no. 640 being the last to West Vale and no. 493 being the last to the Borough Boundary at Birchencliffe.

Just over two years later, on 5 February 1964, the two surviving unrebuilt Karrier MS2 vehicles which retained their original destination indicator layout were requested to perform the last runs on each leg of the no. 60 route. No. 541 was the last to Crosland Hill, whilst no. 544 did the honours on the Birkby section (actually running as a route 10 via Birkby as was the practice for the last run of the day). Both vehicles were widely expected not to run again after this date, but whilst 541 did not do so, your author, bleary eyed after riding on no. 544 the previous night, was amazed to see this latter vehicle pass him in service on Bradford Road as he rode to school. Indeed it ran for another three weeks along with several other trolleybuses that were surplus to requirements after the route 60 conversion.

Another instance of manipulating the identity of the last

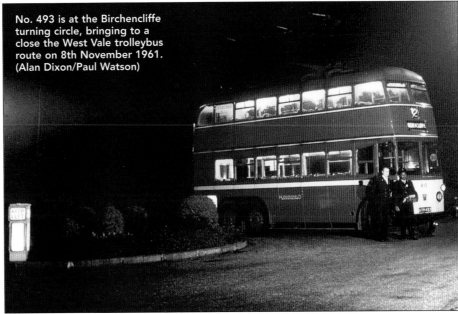

No. 493 is at the Birchencliffe turning circle, bringing to a close the West Vale trolleybus route on 8th November 1961. (Alan Dixon/Paul Watson)

trolleybus occurred for the Almondbury route closure on 14 July 1965. The Huddersfield Trolleybus Preservation Society hoped to purchase no. 593, which was to be withdrawn after this date. Accordingly, it was requested to perform the last run to Almondbury, and this was allowed despite the vehicle having been restricted to peak-hour only working for several weeks due to a weak road spring. Although no. 593 never ran again, due to the difficulty in finding suitable accommodation its preservation was not proceeded with and it met its end in a scrapyard near Leeds.

This is no. 593 (extreme right) awaiting dismantling in a scrapyard at Rothwell near Leeds – not the fate that was originally intended for it. Also in view are (right to left) nos. 578, 588 and 590. (R.F. Mack)

A smart looking no. 600 passes the Market Place. The trailing frog of the connection from Kirkgate is evident above and behind the vehicle. (Fred Ivey)

This portrait of no. 580 shows it at the Fixby stop in Byram Street on a school special journey to Bradley Bar. Note the sign on the shelter: 'Fixby via Bradford Road' visible through the vehicle window. (Fred Ivey)

DISPOSAL OF THE BODIES

The process of separating the unwanted body from its chassis prior to rebuilding and re-bodying of the latter took place at the side of Great Northern Street Works, as depicted here. Some of these bodies were sold to farmers and others for use as storage huts, and could be seen around the town for several years. (A.J. Owen)

One user of these bodies at various times was the Transport Department's sports ground off Leeds Road near Canker Lane. In 1962, the very last body to be discarded, from no. 592, was used as a temporary changing room here. (Author)

As described on page 190, the body of no. 470, preserved following use as a toilet at Epsom, totally collapsed following exposure to high winds. The result is depicted here. (Bruce Lake)

Going home - Lindley-bound passengers board no 626 at Westgate in 1963. It is using the old West Vale stop because of road works at the normal stop further north. Its trolley poles are on the loop wires at this point. (Vic Nutton/Travel Lens Photographic)

Adam Gordon Books

Battery Trams of the British Isles. David Voice, B5, softback, 56pp, £12

Bibliography of British & Irish Tramways. David Croft & Adam Gordon, A4, softback, 486pp, £35

British Tramcar Manufacturers: British Westinghouse and Metropolitan-Vickers. David Voice, B5, softback, 110pp, £16

British Tramway Accidents. F. Wilson, edited by G. Claydon, laminated hardback, 228pp, £35

The Life of Isambard Kingdom Brunel. By his son, reprint of the 1870 edition, softback, 604pp, £20

Treatise upon Cable or Rope Traction. J.Bucknall Smith plus some other literature on that subject, 434pp., all reprints, card covers, limited print run of 125, £45

The Definitive Guide to Trams (including Funiculars) in the British Isles, 3rd edition. D. Voice, softback, A5, 248pp, £20

The Development of the Modern Tram. Brian Patton, hard-backed, 208pp, profusely illustrated in colour, £40

Double-Deck Trams of the World, Beyond the British Isles. B. Patton, A4 softback, 180pp, £18

Double-Deck Trolleybuses of the World, Beyond the British Isles. B. Patton, A4, softback, 96pp, £16

The Douglas Horse Tramway. K. Pearson, softback, 96pp, £14.50

Edinburgh Street Tramways Co. Rules & Regulations. Reprint of 1883 publication, softback, 56pp, £8

Edinburgh's Transport, Vol. 2, The Corporation Years, 1919-1975. D. Hunter, 192pp, softback, £20

Electric Railway Dictionary, definitions and illustrations of the parts and equipment of electric railway cars and trucks. Reprint of 1911 publication by R. Hitt, huge number of figures including numerous very detailed scale drawings, 350pp; hardbacked in buckram, limited print run of 125, £45

Electric Tramway Traction. A. Greatorex (Borough Engineer and Surveyor, West Bromwich), reprint of 1900 original, 92pp, hardbacked in buckram, limited print run of 125, £25

Fell Mountain Railways. Keith Pearson, A4, hardback, 362pp. £45

The Feltham Car of the Metropolitan Electric and London United Tramways. Reprint of 1931 publication, softback, 18pp, £5

Freight on Street Tramways in the British Isles. David Voice, B5, softback, 66pp, £12

The Age of the Horse Tram. David Voice. A4, laminated hard-back, 208pp, £40

Hospital Tramways and Railways, third edition. D. Voice, softback, 108pp, £25

How to Go Tram and Tramway Modelling, third edition. D. Voice, B4, 152pp, completely rewritten, softback, £20

A History of Kingston upon Hull's Tramways. Malcolm Wells, 364pp, laminated hardback, lots of pictures and superb plans compiled by Roger Smith, £50

London County Council Tramways, map and guide to car services, February 1915. Reprint, 12" x 17", folding out into 12 sections, £8

Manx Electric Railway Saga. Robert P. Hendry. A4. Full colour. 144 pp, hardback. £38.80.

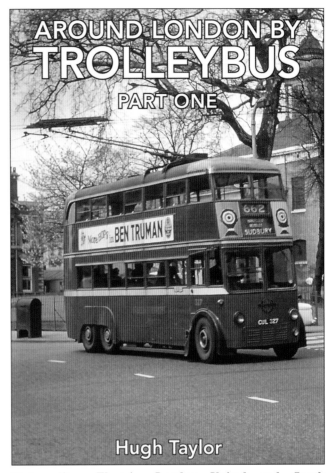

Metropolitan Electric, London United and South Metropolitan Electric Tramways routes map and guide, summer 1925. Reprint, c.14" x 17", folding out into 15 sections, £8

Modern Tramway, reprint of volumes 1 & 2, 1938-1939. A4 cloth hardback, £38

Monorails of the World. D. Voice, A4 softback, 96pp, colour, £25

My 50 Years in Transport. A.G. Grundy, 54pp, softback, 1997, £10

Next Stop Seaton! – 55 Years of Modern Electric Tramways Ltd. Second revised and enlarged edition, D. Jay & D. Voice, B5 softback, 142pp, coloured covers, £20

Omnibuses & Cabs, Their Origin and History. H.C. Moore, hardback reprint with d/w, 282pp, £25

The Overhaul of Tramcars, reprint of LT publication of 1935. 26pp, softback, £6

The History and Development of Steam Locomotion on Common Roads. W. Fletcher, reprint of 1891 edition, soft-back, 332pp, £18

The History of the Steam Tram. H. Whitcombe, hardback, over 60pp, £12

A History of the British Steam Tram, Volume 1. D. Gladwin, hardback, coloured covers, 176pp, 312 x 237mm, profusely illustrated, £40

A History of the British Steam Tram, Volume 2. D. Gladwin, hardback, size as above, coloured covers, 256pp, £40

A History of the British Steam Tram, Volume 3. D. Gladwin, hardback, size as above, coloured covers, 240pp, £45

A History of the British Steam Tram, Volume 4. D. Gladwin, hardback, size as above, coloured covers, 256pp, £45

A History of the British Steam Tram, Volume 5. D. Gladwin, hardback, size as above, coloured covers, 256pp, £45

A History of the British Steam Tram, Volume 6. D. Gladwin, hardback, size as above, coloured covers, 256pp, £45

A History of the British Steam Tram, Volume 7. D. Gladwin, Includes a complete reprint of Some Remarks on Working Street Tramway Lines by Steam Power with Description of Various Engines. By Leonard J. Todd, May 1874. 1008pp in 2 parts, hardbacked, limited print run of 400, £95

Around London by Trolleybus, Part 1. Hugh Taylor, A4 hardback, 184pp, £32

Pontypridd Trolleybuses. David Bowler, A4 hardback, 224pp, £40

Portsmouth Trolleybuses. David Bowler, A4 hardback, 393pp, £48

Railways of Scotland. W. Acworth, reprint of a scarce title of 1890, softback, £15

Shocking Solutions to a Current Problem. how tramways tried to find an alternative to overhead current supply, by David Voice, softback, 125pp, black and white, £16

Street Railways, their construction, operation and maintenance. C.B. Fairchild, reprint of 1892 publication, 496pp, hardback, profusely illustrated, £40

Toy and Model Trams of the World – Volume 1: Toys, die casts and souvenirs. G. Kuře and D. Voice, A4 softback, all colour, 128pp, £25

Toy and Model Trams of the World – Volume 2: Plastic, white metal and brass models and kits. G. Kuře and D. Voice, A4 softback, all colour, 188pp, £30

Trackless to Trolleybus – Trolleybuses in Britain. By Stephen Lockwood, A4, hardbacked, small colour section. £50

George Francis Train's Banquet, report of 1860 on the opening of the Birkenhead tramway. Reprint, softback, 118pp, £10

My Life in Many States and in Foreign Lands. G.F. Train, reprint of his autobiography, softback, over 350pp, £12

Tram and Bus Tokens of the British Isles. David Voice, B5, colour, softback, 66pp, £20

Trams Across the Wear: Remembering Sunderland's Electric Trams. Stephen Lockwood. A4, laminated hardback, 160pp, £35

Trams, Trolleybuses and Buses and the Law before De-regulation. M. Yelton, B4, softback, 108pp, £15

The Tram Driver. by David Tudor, hardbacked, 72pp, £20

Tramway Reflections. David Voice, softback, A4 landscape, all colour, 111 pages; the theme is similar to the Past and Present railway series, showing locations in tramway times and then the same today, £25

Tramway Review, reprint of issues 1-16, 1950-1954. A5 cloth hardback, £23

PORTSMOUTH TROLLEYBUSES

David R.H. Bowler

Published by Adam Gordon

Tramways and Electric Railways in the Nineteenth Century, reprint of Electric Railway Number of Cassier's Magazine, 1899. Cloth hardback, over 250pp, £23

Tramways – Their Construction & Working. D. Kinnear Clark, reprint of the 1894 edition, softback, 812pp, £28

Life of Richard Trevithick. two volumes in one, reprint of 1872 edition, softback, 830pp, £25

The Twilight Years of the Trams in Aberdeen & Dundee. All colour, A4 softback, introduction and captions by A. Brotchie, 120pp, £25

The Twilight Years of the Edinburgh Tram. A4 softback, includes 152 coloured pics, 112pp, £25

The Twilight Years of the Glasgow Tram. Over 250 coloured views, A4, softback, 144 pp, £25

The Wantage Tramway. S.H. Pearce Higgins, with Introduction by John Betjeman, hardback reprint with d/w, over 158pp, £28

The Wearing of the Green, being reminiscences of the Glasgow trams. W. Tollan, softback, 96pp, £12

Works Tramcars of the British Isles. David Voice, B5, softback, 238pp, £25

ADAM GORDON
Kintradwell Farmhouse, Brora, Sutherland KW9 6LU
Tel: 01408 622660 E-mail: adam@ahg-books.com Website: www.ahg-books.com